THE ENCHANTMENTS OF JUDAISM
Rites of Transformation from Birth to Death

SOUTH FLORIDA STUDIES IN THE HISTORY OF JUDAISM

Edited by
Jacob Neusner
William Scott Green, James Strange

Number 21
The Enchantment of Judaism
Rites of Transformation from Birth Through Death

by
Jacob Neusner

THE ENCHANTMENTS OF JUDAISM
Rites of Transformation from Birth Through Death

Second Printing

by

Jacob Neusner

Scholars Press
Atlanta, Georgia

THE ENCHANTMENTS OF JUDAISM
Rites of Transformation from Birth to Death

Publication of this book was made possible by a grant from the Tisch Family Foundation, New York City. The University of South Florida acknowledges with thanks this important support for its scholarly projects.

Library of Congress Cataloging in Publication Data

Neusner, Jacob, 1932-
    The enchantments of Judaism : rites of transformation from birth
    through death / by Jacob Neusner.
    p. cm. — (South Florida studies in the history of Judaism ;
    no. 21)
    Reprint. Originally published: New York : Basic Books, c1987.
    Includes bibliographical references and index.
    ISBN 1-55540-589-4 (acid-free paper)
    1. Judaism—Customs and practices—Meditations. 2. Jewish way of
life—Meditations. I. Title. II. Series: South Florida studies in
the history of Judaism ; 21.
[BM700.N48 1991]
296.7'4—dc20   91-118
                                   CIP

Printed in the United States of America
on acid-free paper

∞

In memory of

Abraham Joshua Heschel.

Every day that passes vindicates his life and faith

and

his hope for Judaism in America and for America.

CONTENTS

[vii]

Contents

PREFACE

JUDAISM takes everyday and ordinary experiences and transforms them through prayer and rite—and, with them, ourselves as Jews—into metaphors for the sacred: an enchantment through rite, "in our image, after our likeness." To gentiles who want to understand how eternity echoes in the lives of their Jewish friends and neighbors, as it does in Christian life as well, and to Jews who seek to grasp how they in their everyday encounter with ordinary life form part of that sacred society that is Israel, the Jewish people, I offer this book.

The occasion is a familiar one: a question about why the Jews are not like the Christians and how the Jews are religious at all. A close friend and great scholar, a Lutheran minister teaching at a Roman-Catholic university, commented that his Jewish students seemed to him deeply secular. I asked, "But do they come to class on the Day of Atonement?"

He: "No, not one."

I: "To your knowledge, do many of them attend a Passover *seder*?"

He: "All of them, to the last one."

I: "And did they demonstrate last month for Soviet Jewry?"

He: "How did you know?"

I: "And are they concerned about Israel—that is, the State of Israel?"

He: "It matters, it matters."

Preface

As we shall see, the Day of Atonement, the Passover *seder,* the marriage ceremony, the burial rite, these and other celebrations of home and family matter to the vast majority of Jewish Americans and Canadians, West Europeans, Brazilians and Argentinians, Australians and South Africans. The political issues of Jewish corporate life, typified by work in behalf of Soviet Jewry and concern with the State of Israel, engages the same vast majority, inspiring vivid energies, deep emotions. The one set of rites derives, as I shall explain, from the Judaism of the dual Torah; the other, from the Judaism of Holocaust and Redemption.

These two Judaisms, each with its symbolic system and appeal to a story of who *we* are and what on that account *we* must do, coexist side by side in the lives of the middle range of Jewry. In the hearts of Jews of Reform, Conservative, middle-class Orthodox, Reconstructionist,*or, for that matter, humanist commitment—whether those Jews are members of a synagogue or unaffiliated—these two Judaisms evoke profound and life-transforming affections, attitudes, and emotions. The one serves home and family; the other, the corporate community. A simple statement of their ubiquity suffices. When one Jew marries another Jew, it is virtually unheard of for them to have a civil, not a Judaic, religious marriage—a rite that derives from the Judaism of the dual Torah. The sign

---

*Reconstructionism is the fourth movement within American Judaism, in addition to the Reform, Orthodox, and Conservative Judaisms. Growing out of the theology of Mordecai M. Kaplan, Reconstructionism, with its Reconstructionist rabbinical college in Philadelphia, teaches that God is the power that makes for salvation, and develops the idea of a this-worldly and naturalist definition of God. Reconstructionism further speaks of the importance of Jewish peoplehood and community and affirms Judaic religious practices as expressions of all that is good and holy in that peoplehood. The movement broke off from Conservative Judaism, but the ideas of Kaplan have influenced many rabbis, Reform and Conservative alike.

of the other Judaism, that of Holocaust and Redemption, proves equally one-sided: deep concern for the State of Israel, profound response to the tale of the destruction of European Jewry between 1933 and 1945. When we discern the power and influence of these two Judaisms and understand how they work, we shall see how and why Jewish Americans and Canadians, West Europeans, Brazilians and Argentinians, Australians and South Africans constitute—in varying ways, to be sure—a singular people on earth.

I do not deal with that small segment of the Jewish-American world who find their way to the synagogue twice a day, study the Torah morning and night, live out their lives wholly within the Judaism of the dual Torah. That sector of Jewry, self-segregated and rightly self-assured, raises no questions about religiosity. It is pious in the profound and rich sense of Judaism. Synagogues of that sector of Jewry, mostly Orthodox, are crowded on weekdays and require two or three or more worship services on the Sabbath. While these Jews (in the main) remain aloof from the appeal of Holocaust and Redemption, for them Judaism encompasses the whole of life and commitment; and both the private and the familial, and also the civic and the public, life of Jewry join in a single entity, defined within the Torah in two parts, oral and written, which God handed over to Moses at Mount Sinai. No study has suggested that the observant Orthodox compose so much as one tenth of the Jews of North America; though in a few major cities, such as New York City or London, the proportion is perhaps double. The bulk of Jewish Americans, Canadians, West Europeans, Latin Americans, South Africans, and Australians do not live within the disciplines of the Torah. While in North America most of the Jews (nonobservant in the Orthodox sense) do not affiliate with the Orthodox community, they do in Western Europe and the European communities of South Africa and Australia; but the picture does not change. Jews integrated into the values and civilization of the West have a dual Judaism—the one for the home, the other for the life of public discourse; and it is that Judaism that shapes and defines the lives of nearly all Jews in the West, those who are not fully observant in the Orthodox definition.

But it would be a mistake to see as fundamentally secular ordinary Jewish Jewish Americans and Canadians and West Europeans, Brazilians and Argentinians, Australians and South Africans, living not in segregation but culturally wholly integrated among their gentile, mostly Christian neighbors. I shall show that these Jews—like their neighbors in some ways, unlike them in others—respond to the crises of life and history by invoking a very particular story of who they are. This story speaks not of mere facts but talks of God's actions and demands. Thus, in secular America and Canada dwells a people who, in the inner vision of heart and soul, in moments dwells alone in splendid encounter with God. Integrated in clothing and language, commonly in food and neighborhood, in work and rest, are God's people; and, in their own way, these Canadians and Americans listen to God's voice and so act as to sanctify the lives together that God has given to them.

I offer here, then, a liturgical theology of Judaism—the second, so far as I know, attempted in our times. The first was Heschel's.

Let me explain. Nearly forty years ago, it was from Abraham Joshua Heschel that I learned to try to understand Judaism through liturgical theology. His book *The Sabbath: Its Meaning for Modern Man,* published in 1948,[1] came to the office of the newspaper my father had founded and then published, the *Connecticut Jewish Ledger.* I was then a high school student,

Preface

sixteen years old, working every afternoon and weekends as errand boy; but, fathers and sons being what they are, my father told me to write editorials when our editor was away, to do the news, the headlines, the layout—and, by the way, to review the books that came in. So I did. Heschel's book came to the office, and I read it, as I read pretty much anything else that came my way. It was different from anything I had ever read, and I have never seen anything like it since. The reason is that Heschel moved from the here and the now to the holy, appealing to the world as it is as—in the language I use here—metaphor and simile for the real world of God. I had never heard anyone talk about Judaism that way. I had never known that Judaism in its practices (to which, as a Reform Jew, I had scarcely been exposed) had anything to do with God, in whom I believed; or with "being Jewish," which was then as now definitive of, critical to, my very being— whatever that might be. I reviewed the book, and said so. I wrote to Heschel (I always write to the author of a book that has changed me, or, if the author is dead, at least in my mind call the author up on the phone and conduct an imaginary conversation), and he wrote back.

Some years later, Heschel received me as a student at the Jewish Theological Seminary of America and more than once spoke with me about *The Sabbath,* saying that the same book can and should be written about every detail of the life of Judaism. It is only appropriate, therefore, that I offer this book in his memory, even though I cannot claim that I realize the goal he set for me, let alone continue the work he began in what was and is, I believe, the single most powerful and important book on the living reality of Judaism ever written in the English language. But that is how things are, from one generation to the next: we are what we are. My questions lead

[xiii]

not to advocacy but, I hope, to insight: *I want to know why things work as they do and not in some other way.* In this book I explain which rites work and which do not, and then why this, not that.

I am a historian of religion, concentrating on Judaism, not a theologian such as Heschel was. Nonetheless this is a theological book, written on the border between the history of religion and theology, and I take utterly unwarranted pride when, in a fit of exaggeration, someone compliments me with the title of theologian. But it is not entirely inappropriate to my intention. For, in studying the history of religion, exemplified by Judaism, I have now come to the end of the "out there" work of description, analysis, and interpretation in the framework of society and culture—that is, the study of religion in this world. In this book, I propose to move from history into the "in here" realm of theology. True, the incursion is only brief. And the problems I have defined for future work will not yield further inquiries such as this book suggests; I remain what I always was, a historian of religion, working on Judaism.

In two recent works of mine, *Self-Fulfilling Prophecy: Exile and Return in the History of Judaism* (1987) and *Death and Birth of Judaism* (1987), I presented, respectively, an encompassing theory of the history of Judaism over its entire trajectory, and a description of the way any Judaism comes into being and grows, blossoms, bears fruit, and (at least, some Judaisms) withers and dies.[2] I here offer a complementary statement: that is, I wish now to speak not of the plant in its unfolding life cycle but of the blossom and the fruit. I mean to appreciate and enjoy the fragrance and the flavor of Judaism: no longer *a* Judaism, but the one living Judaism defined by the Torah, written and oral, revealed by God at Sinai to Moses, our rabbi, as Orthodoxy, Reform, Conservative, Reconstructionist, and all other Judaic systems of continuation and renewal continue that Judaism of the dual Torah. There, in the Torah, enchantment through the working of our imagination and the power of our intention transforms mere words into that entire world of rebirth and regeneration that each of us—in life and death and in life to come, under God's rule and with God's grace—renews.

It is time.

—JACOB NEUSNER
Purim 5747
15 March 1987

The Enchantments of Judaism

Enchantment
through Words

RELIGION reaches each of us—Jew or gentile—through words, and of them makes worlds, realms of enchantment, of transcendence. The history of religion, in dwelling on what religion is and does in culture and society and politics, on how it has shaped the life of this world, tells us everything but what we want to know. Students of religion seek in their subject not only understanding but also faith and truth. While these the history of religion, in its nature, does not claim to reveal, another cognitive science, theology, does so claim. From the history of religion—in my case, Judaism—I move, therefore, to theology—a move leading straight and true from that history, whose social and cultural dimensions of this-worldly human experiences have, since the beginning of history, precipitated theological reflection on the world of the spirit beyond. Judaic theology sees human beings as both metaphor and simile: "in our image, after our likeness," as God said of Adam; and to construct a theology of Judaism is to explore the meaning of humanity viewed as image and likeness of something else, of life lived as metaphor: an ongoing existence of *as if.*

In describing, analyzing and comparing, and interpreting religion in history, we study the things—made of words, pigment, stone—that people have left as testimonies to faith. Like many who take up the study of religion, I want to know not only the this-worldly testimony but the object of that testimony: the reality of God in the life of Judaism, not alone the meaning of the words that point to or convey the reality. Where, I wonder—beyond and within the evidences of religion in the here and now—is God within and beyond? Thus, I seek to understand what study about the subject cannot teach. But understanding rests on learning, and faith seeks intelligence. A religious world without words to tell us in proposition and syllogism what is at hand lives only for the moment of its epiphany. But a religious world composed only of words to tell us misleads and deludes, as does a kiss through a veil, a poem in translation, a report about pain, a narrative of someone else's death.

I have studied about religion, exemplified by Judaism, since before I reached the age of *mitzvot,* at thirteen, to now, more than four decades later. But, after studying many sacred texts and writing more than two hundred books about Judaism, I have found still open the question with which I began: God's question to Man and Woman, Where are you?—now addressed to God. In studying about religion, in the case of Judaism or any other religion, we take up the testimonies that in words propose to convey that world of God that answers the human question framed in Scripture by God. The history of religion responds to God's question to us—Where are you?—by telling us about humanity, our quest for God. Studying religion brings us, therefore, to the outer limits of this-worldly evidence for the world within and beyond—the realm of God. In simple language, the history of religion leads to the border of theology. In this book, I cross that frontier and propose to answer that other question, the one we ask, as Scripture defines the question, of God: Where are you?

Who is the *I* who speaks? Who is the *you* to whom I speak? I grew up in a Reform Temple; went to the Conservative rabbinical school, the Jewish Theological Seminary of America; studied with a tutor in the Orthodox yeshiva, Mir, in Jerusalem and at the Hebrew University; was raised in a Zionist home in West Hartford, Connecticut. I find value and meaning in every Judaism. And while I speak to everyone interested in Judaism, either as an example of religion or as the one religion of personal engagement, my immediate audience is the Reform, Conservative, or nonobservant Jew confronted by the reality of living Judaism and uncertain how to respond. I mean to explain, not exhort; to interpret, not to inveigh. I aim to open many doors to the world of the religious life of Judaism and to close but one, the one that leads backward, to a world without enchantment, to a life without regeneration and renewal.

Of what Judaism do I speak? I appeal to the lived and experienced Judaism of the everyday liturgy. That is where I find the words of enchantment that effect the transformation of the everyday into metaphor and simile. The liturgy addresses the commonplace and perceives the remarkable, transforms the routine into event. That liturgy presents the words we say to accomplish the transformation from the here and the now to the metaphor and model of God beyond, the simile of God within: in our image, after our likeness. A believing and practicing Jew, I claim here to speak of Judaism in broad and encompassing terms, so that whether Orthodox or Reform, Conservative or Reconstructionist, every other believing and practicing Jew will find in my account of enchantment

[5]

and transformation something that actually happens or can happen to her or to him. As in *Death and Birth of Judaism,* I find myself sympathetic to all Judaisms but empathetic to none. The reason I believe I may address everyone is that I invoke those rites of enchantment, moments of transformation, that are common to all Jews within all Judaic systems of the day. These are for nearly all Jews universal modes of reforming the here and now into paradigms of eternity. In occasions of enchantment, the locative is transformed into the utopian, the one-time into the all-the-time, the private person into Israel, the individual into Adam or Eve. So I discover that, in the consecrated moment, I am no longer where I thought I was but somewhere else, I am no longer who I thought I was but something more, I live no longer in one finite moment but in a different time. Transformed by the power of Judaism, I become other than what I seemed to be—and so do we all.

No act of enchantment that I invoke as evidence for the power of Judaism to transform and reconstruct will present itself as alien or unknown to any believing and practicing Jew, whether Reform or Hasidic or Yeshiva-Orthodox or Modern-Orthodox (though I myself am closer to the Reform than the Hasidic, and closest to the center), whether a proud child of the Exile or a fulfilled daughter or son of the Land and State of Israel (though, without apology or regret, I live in the Exile). I believe that the universal Judaism displayed in this book is one of the vital and powerful religions of the living world; and that its power and vitality lie in the act of creation through which, as in God's creation of the world, words are transformed into worlds, in the here and now, through enchantment. It is through such enchantment that ordinary human experiences are transformed into metaphors of the sacred, enchantment being called, in the language of Judaism, "sanctification." Just as God created Man and Woman "in our image, after our likeness," so, I argue, we stand for something more, as metaphor, as simile: like God. And this we do in most concrete reality, for each human experience is a simile of the sacred and serves as a metaphor for the transformation of the given into a gift of God. Thus, in the ordinary moments of everyday life (as I review in part I)—whether going from hunger to satisfaction or having a baby or getting married—each of us finds himself or herself treated as metaphor for something beyond the individual, yet deep within our experience. Again, those rites that address us as a *we*—first a family, then a community—turn us into something else than what we see (as I review in part II). That is what I mean by enchantment that changes us from what we are to something more. Judaism as a religion treats life *as if:* that is, through imagination it transforms the ordinary experience of *is* into the holy. This transformation tells us, in the material moments of the workaday world, what it means to be in God's image, after His likeness—tells us, indeed, what He is made of.

I argue in favor of three propositions. The first is that words have power. Rightly spoken with proper intention, coming from the heart, words bring forth worlds, through enchantment turning the everyday into something remarkable—the enchantment of heart and soul and mind, which comes to expression in deed turned into gesture. A commonplace deed may be to light a candle. A gesture is to kindle a flame to inaugurate the Sabbath. A deed is to eat a cracker. A gesture is to raise a piece of unleavened bread—a cracker of a certain kind—and to announce that it is the bread that our ancestors ate when they hastily left Egypt—and then to eat the cracker. Enchantment reaches fulfillment in the transformation of the here and now of the everyday into the then and there of life with the living God. Enchantment engages the given of our lives and transforms that into a gift.

But, second, some words of Judaism so work as to make worlds of meaning only in a particular circumstance: that is, in the Judaism that thrives in America and Canada, Western Europe and Latin America, South Africa and Australia, when words speak to the individual and to the family. Lacking the experience of religion lived in a corporate community, people find it difficult to enter into, let alone transform, those social worlds of Judaism that transcend the private life. People appeal, when at home, to one set of rites and their accompanying myths—stories explaining the truth—and respond, when in community, to another set of rites and myths, telling a different story altogether. The private life and home are changed by rite into holy places. The shared life of the community, lived with other Jews, is not commonly changed by words deriving from the same origin. But the life of the corporate community, too, is transformed into heightened being, made to refer to experience and value not materially present. When words speak of me, my life and my family, they transform; when they speak of us, all Israel, all together, in the language of the holy, the same words fall away unheard. But other words—not deriving from the dual Torah, written and oral, that constitutes God's revelation to Israel—the Jewish people invoke, evoke, provoke, transform. Those other words do change us, as profoundly and as completely as do the words of the rites of the dual Torah. The same tears come, but the music is different.

And, third, another set of words work for those same Jews, words that—as I shall explain in chapter 1—make a different world from the one formed of imaginary Israel in the family of Abraham, Isaac, and Jacob. Those other words form a separate Judaism from the one evoked for individual and family on those rites of passage nearly universally observed. The corporate community unchanged by the words of one Judaism comes into being through the power of the words of a different Judaism. I identify that other Judaism and explain why in the context of the religious life of Jewries throughout the free world, where Jews are free to practice any Judaism of their choice or none, the nature of religion in general leads to the formation of the two Judaisms—one for the private life of home and family, the other for the political life of the community and its public policy—that today flourish. So I claim to explain why this, not that, in the life of Judaism today in North America and Latin America, Western Europe, South Africa, and Australia.

Two vast Jewries lie beyond my claim to understanding. The one, in the Soviet empire, to us is locked away and inaccessible. The other, in the State of Israel, lives out an existence in political, therefore also social and cultural, facts utterly unlike those of us in the Diaspora, or *Golah* ("exile"). I cannot pretend to understand and explain what Judaisms work or do not work, how they change and how they do not affect, the Jews of those vast communities. The Judaisms at work in the State of Israel and in the Jewry of the Soviet empire demand description, analysis, and explanation, too. But, while I believe the questions I ask pertain, I cannot pretend to explain what I do not understand.

In speaking of the power of words to form worlds, the strength of the imagination to define reality, I turn to the liturgical life of the Judaism that all Jews know: Grace after Meals, circumcision, the marriage ceremony called the *huppah,* the Passover banquet meal called the *seder,* the ineffable power of the prayers for the New Year, Rosh Hashanah, and the Day of Atonement, Yom Kippur. I further invoke the equally affecting liturgy of Sabbaths and festivals, and, above all, the daily prayer of the *Shema,* the Eighteen Benedictions, and the *Alenu.* I try to explain why the former set of liturgies exercise power nearly universally, while the latter ones—Sabbath and daily prayer—do not. In appealing to the contents of the liturgies of Judaism to explain why some rites enjoy currency, others decay, I treat as socially important the theological propositions of Judaism. And I further maintain that the contents respond to the context as well. This analysis of the theological power of Judaism in its received form and of the presently definitive strength of a competing Judaism appeals to the interplay of contents and context, text and matrix. Yet the simple premise of this book is that the liturgy of Judaism *is* Judaism, so far as we understand by "Judaism" a religion comprising a world view and a way of life formed in the discipline of God's will for humanity.

Parts I and II show how enchantment works through celebration and story to transform both the individual and the group, respectively: how I, and we, come to stand not alone for myself, or ourselves, but for much else, for more than I, or we, have imagined. Thus, part I specifically discusses how in a simple meal, in the birth of a baby, in marriage, I am not *where* I think I am, but somewhere else, not *when* I think I am, but in another time altogether, and not *who* I think I am, but someone else altogether. Then part II turns to how the Passover *seder,* the Sabbath and the festivals, and the Days of Awe similarly transform us as a group into a wholly other entity: more than we thought we were, much more.

But, in Judaic existence, there is only here and now, the moment at which I am only what I am and nothing more. In addition to the *bar* or *bat mitzvah,* at least one reality is left unwashed by transforming worlds: the reality of the corpse, my moment of death. There the world falls silent, not subject to enchantment and transformation into something other than what it seems to be. The dirt is real; the body, a mere corpse. Then Judaism in its received statement effects—and this without words but solely in affirmation of God's rule—its most profound wonder of transformation, for the corpse, yet a corpse, in God's realm lives. The words that do not invoke another world and fail at the task of transformation conceal enchantment beyond all imagining. This is the message of part III.

In part IV, I turn to the social world of the synagogue, the concrete realm of worship. There are two propositions in this part: one concerns the power of theological expression contained within synagogue worship; the other explains why that power exercises so little charm for Jews that the synagogues stand empty most of the year. While in the synagogue words evoke a world of meaning specifically on those few occasions when they address the self, on Sabbaths and on festivals Israel as holy society listens to different words from those of the synagogue, responds to a different Judaism from the Judaism of the synagogue liturgy. But I think that ultimately, as I shall come to in my epilogue, there is a way to allow words to form not only worlds but one world encompassing all Israel in the here and now.

My fundamental thesis is that we are changed by what happens in our hearts and minds and souls. That is to say, we are Jews through the power of imagination. And imagination takes shape in response to words we find compelling. Self-evidently, by *words* I mean not only statements made in intellectual form but also the messages of sound and silence, movement and gesture, touch and sight, all the signals of our senses. Our inner vision, our power to create out of the resources of heart and mind and soul—from these sources of intellect and sensibility alone flow our sense of ourselves as individuals and as part of a corporate society: Israel, the Jewish people. We are what we imagine ourselves to be. We live by asking, What if? and why? and why not?—acts of imagination all.

Let me give a single example of the life of imagination that makes us Jews. The greatest Jewish experience comes to us in our mind's eye: the Passover *seder,* where we are told to see ourselves *as if*—"as if we are slaves freed from Egyptian bondage." That is an act of imagination, and it represents the many other acts of surpassing imagination that make us what we are. But it is only one. When we get married, we pretend we are Adam and Eve in Eden. When we perform the rite of circumcision, we set a chair for the prophet Elijah. When we say *kaddish* and *Yizkor* (the prayer of remembrance for the dead), we see in our imagination worlds not present, but worlds without end: God's kingdom, God's rule.

To state matters simply: to be a Jew (and, I would claim, to be a human being—for everyone can say what I here say of Jewry in particular) is to become what in mind and heart and soul we imagine that we are. Thus to be a Jew is an act of art: that is, of imagination and creation; of making ourselves out of ourselves. And, it follows, to be a Jew is to become more than what in everyday reality we think we are—each one of us in the appropriate medium of voice or gesture or word or mime, in the medium of the stage or the street, in the language of words or of color and shape or of an imagined persona. To be a Jew is to become what in our power of imagination we make of ourselves. To be a Jew is, therefore, an act of will; and will wells up from within: an act of imagination. Words make worlds within—and then we change the world.

CHAPTER 1

The World Out There: Contemporary Judaism

The general phenomenon of ritual is no mere squelching of emotion, no cage of the feelings. Rather, we have to do with a cognitive ordering of categories of time, space, action, and community.
—ISRAEL SCHEFFLER

IN RELIGION words serve as do the notes in music. The musical notes are not the music and do not make the music. The musician makes the music, guided by—responding to— the notes. The two violinists, the violist, and the cellist of the quartet form the silences, define the rhythm, therefore also create the logic and power of the sound. The notes do not make the music; the musician-artists make the music. To that never-to-be-predicted moment of transformation of time into rhythm and sound into melody and harmony, and of those present into an audience engaged in witness and response, the musical notes on paper are necessary but never suffice. So, too, in religion, God made the world with words. But the words are not the world: they are necessary but not sufficient. The religious community—in this case, Israel, the holy people of

God—turn the words into a sacred and consecrated world. The words transform; the world is what is changed.* The words of religion do not make religion. Religious people make religion, in the language of religion, through God's grace and intervention, in the language of this-worldly description: through an act of will and faith and, above all, judgment and intellect and imagination, artists of religion make religion as artists of music make music. God or the composer—creators above or below—send out the words, the notes, to those who will receive them and make something of them. And while not all of us can make music, all of us are, or can be, artists in religion: creators of worlds.

Words do their work when they work a wonder and change me and us all into something different from, and more than what I and we imagine, so that the life of Judaism is the encounter with, the experience of the mind's enchantment and the inner transformation of sensibility and imagination. In the Judaism practiced in Latin and North America, Australia, South Africa, and Western Europe, however, we take for granted that the religious life works itself out mainly in words. In working out its common life through public debate, writing and reading and discourse of thought, the Judaism of the West reduces the worlds of sustaining inner nurture to exercises in transactions, to exchanges of words. Judaism in its moments of practical engagement in the life of the synagogue and community treats as critical propositions of belief or nonbelief, rather than attitudes of trust and submission, acceptance and inner encounter. Feelings, expressed in sound and sight, sympathy and empathy, conveyed in gesture and motion and movement—these take second place, where they are admitted at all.

*To this argument the debate on the role of intellect in ritual is not pertinent.

The World Out There: Contemporary Judaism

The rivers of unfelt words that drown sensibility and sentiment in the right circumstance may nourish life. It is true, as the philosopher Israel Scheffler insists, that in rite we deal with the cognitive ordering of categories of time, space, action, and community.[1] Yet ritual is not mere cognition, nor does rite work only or mainly through hearing and understanding words. Indeed, quite the opposite: the reworking of the givens of the world into a new construction of meaning may take place through circumstance, without regard to word. Who can be moved by these legalistic words, stated in a formula as if before a judge in a court of law:

> All vows and oaths we take, all promises and obligations we make between this Day of Atonement and the next we hereby publicly retract in the event that we should forget them and hereby declare our intention to be absolved of them.

Sung at sunset on the eve of the Day of Atonement, the formula called *Kol Nidre* (for the opening words, "All vows"), scarcely understood for the trivial pledge it contains, moves masses of Jews to come to synagogue who otherwise seldom find their way there. Hardly poetry, this passage, sung in the synagogue, before the open empty Ark, with the scrolls of the Torah held before the congregation in the arms of its leaders, marks the single transforming, enchanting moment in the synagogue year. So it is not the mere words. But words do matter. For what the formula, sung in high drama, conveys is the proposition, entirely cognitive in content, that we sin but may atone, that God judges but will forgive. The power of the *Kol Nidre* flows not from the words but from the setting, and the setting comes about because of the drama—staging, choreog-

[15]

raphy, song—formed by the presence of the audience in the theater of a drama of life and death: Who will live? who will die? who by fire? who by water?

Knowing the power of the synagogue to tap deep wells of passion, to lay before the assembled individuals the reality of community and to convoke community and invoke God's presence, we should expect the synagogues to be crowded from week to week. But (except for a sector of Orthodoxy) they are not. For the enchantment of poetry gives way to the boredom of repetition; and drama as an exchange of power in voice and word and tableau, theater as a world of enchantment and transformation, the arts as means of speaking beyond words and besides words—these modes of expression of inner reality come under neglect. Consequently, that reality in which the soul lives—and it is the soul that, within us, is like God—finds itself set aside in the synagogue, where it should sustain. Judaism—meant to tell us that we are more than what we seem, that we take place elsewhere as well as here and now, and live longer than death—that Judaism of a world beyond and a world within does not work its enchantment when it should. As a result, the synagogue—where we become other, more than what we think we are; where we specifically turn into holy Israel, God's people—does not change its members into the holy other, the holy congregation of God. Instead, all things are made one thing. Words, aimed not at heart but at mind, are meant not to invoke, evoke, provoke, call from deep to deep—but only to reduce reality to proposition, feeling and sensibility to syllogism, all things to the one thing represented by that small corner of the mind furnished with the hard and single shapes of words. That is why there is so little silence, when enchantment can take place, and so much public discourse about something of which no one has actual experience.

The World Out There: Contemporary Judaism

The word *liturgy* comes from a Greek word that means "labor," just as the Hebrew word for "divine service," *abodah,* also means "work." The work of the service of the heart is owing; it is part of what religion, in this case Judaism, rightly requires. But words do not and cannot create worlds when prayer serves only as laborious liturgy, when study of Torah is replaced by sermons, when—if we attend "services" at all— all things are done as other than the holy service to God.

The liturgy of the North American synagogue in the East European tradition, for example, suppresses dance, though there are processionals; sidesteps symbol, though symbols, pictorial and mime alike, are present in abundance; and treats singing as casual and individual, though the Torah—the scrolls of Scripture—is proclaimed through song and hymns, and prayers are sung. The motionless repetition of words predominates, an endless repetition, reducing poetry not to prose but to mere repetition and incantation. No wonder people subside into themselves and mumble in solitary. In synagogue prayer today, drama, dance, music, display of evocative symbol, the opportunity for renewal and regeneration of the holy community—the word of God, the word to God—both are buried under an avalanche of words. And yet, as I shall show in the shank of this book, in the Judaism of the American and Canadian and European synagogue, words are there meant to create worlds. Words form worlds that tell me I am someone else, instruct me I am somewhere else, move me from this place, this time, to an enchanted world of eternity. Sometimes words make worlds, enchant and transform us ordinary people into the extraordinary people, Israel. Oftentimes they do not; people do not want them to.

The reason is that, misunderstanding the true nature of religion, we take for granted that religion, in this case Judaism, works mainly in words. And that is quite natural. For we refer to Scripture or even to God as the Word (for God, *Memra*); and as intellectuals, scholars, and theologians, we also receive Scripture as an exercise in words, whether historical facts or doctrines of faith. But religion works not in but only through words—as these form only one medium among media. For God speaks from heart to heart and soul to soul, not only mind to mind, and asks for not only belief in given propositions (on which, as a matter of fact, we religious people may differ) but for faith and trust (in Hebrew, *emunah*) on which we religious people all concur. It follows, therefore, that through Torah or Scripture God speaks in many voices, only a few of them forming words, phrases, sentences, propositions.

Scripture's stories form pictures, appeal to symbols, speak like a subtle quartet through silences as much as sound: *like a hammer that strikes the anvil.* Not only so, but Scripture is sung in the synagogue, proclaimed as music, not only words. There is another world beyond the words of paraphrase, prophecy, or parable, a world of profound and encompassing meaning conveyed when words fall back: art and music, sensibility and sentiment, as much as intellect and syllogism. The Torah, God's word, affects feelings and attitudes and reaches expression in different media from words alone or mainly. Through enchantment, transformation of the ordinary so takes place that new worlds of meaning, new realms of being, come about. Words speak to—therefore, for—the mind. But through enchantment, words bring to life this other world of meaning altogether; the world of vision and form, of sound and feeling and gesture, of movement and stillness, speaks to—and, therefore, for—the imagination, which, in God and humanity alike, flourishes in soul and in heart and in spirit. If "man does not live by bread alone but by all things that come from God's mouth," then God, for God's part, does not speak by words alone. Both find being in soul and heart and spirit, in feeling, and in imagination and not only in intellect. In the realm reached when words fail but life endures, Israel lives, and so does God.

All that I have said presupposes that there is a *we,* a group of Jews joined by shared attitudes and norms. To some that may appear self-evident. But others may look at Jews in the West and see only white, secular, generally middle-class Western women and men. Or they may identify Jews as different only in private, and not in public. So let me briefly show that Jews do form a community beyond the family and home, so that we may appeal to a shared public experience, a polity in common, in our call for an everyday to be changed into another world. Those indicative traits that point toward social continuity and corporate cohesion in point of fact encompass social processes such as marriage and family formation, residence and mobility, social class, occupation, education, economic status, communal affiliation, and identification and behavior. Family, stratification of Jewish society, and diverse characteristics of ethnicity—all mark the Jews as a group distinctive in their larger social setting. So, too, as the sociologist and demographer Calvin Goldscheider says, "There are critical links between family and stratification, between social class and migration, between jobs, residence, education, family, and ethnicity." Goldscheider's and others' studies have shown that the Jews form a distinctive social group, with the indicators of difference sharply etched and well framed:

A detailed examination of family, marriage, childbearing, social class, residence, occupation and education among Jews and non-Jews leads to the unmistakable conclusion that

Jews are different. Their distinctiveness as a community is further reinforced by religious and ethnic forms of cohesiveness. . . . Jewish exceptionalism means more than the absence of assimilation. The distinctive features of American Jewish life imply bonds and linkages among Jews which form the multiple bases of communal continuity. These ties are structural as well as cultural; they reflect deeply embedded forms of family, educational, job and residence patterns, reinforced by religious and ethnic-communal behavior, cemented by shared lifestyles and values.[2]

These humble facts have little to do with our exalted themes, enchantment and transformation. But if change is to take place, it is because a group of people waits to be transformed. And the traits of the group set forth the arena, and limits, of transformation: from this to that, in a world of limited possibilities.

That group shares life, believes something in common, endures a collective fate and condition, wants the same things and hopes for them. Religion is public, not private, something we do together, not a belief or an idea that I have on my own, or you on your own. That is why when we wish to understand the Judaisms among us, we begin with a clear statement of why we think there is an *us* to be described. So much for the fact that Jews in the United States and Canada constitute a profoundly united and amply differentiated community. There is a shared corporate experience of polity, which is distinctive to Jewry at large and transcends genealogy, on the one side, and individual taste and judgment and belief, on the other.

Two Judaisms flourish, as I have said, in the vast middle range of the socially integrated Jewries of the West: one for home and family; one for the shared life of the corporate community. The Judaism found compelling in the private life derives from the Judaism of the dual Torah, oral and written, that took shape in late antiquity, the first seven centuries of the Common Era, and reached its definitive statement in the Talmud of Babylonia. That Judaism not only flourished, as the normative and paramount system, into the nineteenth century but now, on the eve of the twenty-first, continues to impart shape and structure to the ongoing life of the synagogue, to its liturgy, its holy days and festivals, its theology, its way of life and world view. The second Judaism came on the scene only in the aftermath of the Second World War and the rise of the State of Israel. I call this the "Judaism of Holocaust and Redemption," because it is a Judaic system that invokes, as its generative world view, the catastrophe of the destruction by Germany of most of the Jews of Europe between 1933 and 1945 and the creation, three years afterward, of the State of Israel. This Judaism, too, has its way of life, its religious duties, its public celebrations. It is communal, stressing public policy and practical action. It involves political issues; for example, policy toward the State of Israel, government assistance in helping Soviet Jews gain freedom, and, in the homelands of the Jewish Americans or Canadians or Britons or French, matters of local politics as well. The first of the two Judaisms flourishes in the synagogue, as I have said; and the second, in the streets. The one is private, the other public; the one personal and familial, the other civic and communal.

Let me spell out the world view and way of life of that other Judaism, which has the power to transform civic and public affairs in Jewry as much as the Judaism of the dual Torah enchants and changes the personal and familial ones. In politics, history, society, Jews in North America respond to the Judaism of the Holocaust and Redemption in such a way as to imagine they are someone else, living somewhere else, at another time and circumstance. That vision transforms families into an Israel, a community. The somewhere else is Poland in 1944 and the earthly Jerusalem, and the vision turns them from reasonably secure citizens of America or Canada into insecure refugees finding hope and life in the Land and State of Israel. Public events commemorate, so that *we* were there in "Auschwitz," which stands for all of the centers where Jews were murdered; and *we* share, too, in the everyday life of that faraway place in which we do not live but should, the State of Israel. That transformation of time and of place, no less than the recasting accomplished by the Passover *seder* or the rite of *berit milah* or the *huppah,* turns people into something other than what they are in the here and now.

The issues of this public Judaism, the civil religion of North American Jewry (and not theirs alone), are perceived to be political. But the power of that Judaism to turn things into something other than what they seem, to teach lessons that change the everyday into the remarkable—that power works no less wonderfully than does the power of the other Judaism to make me Adam or one of the Israel who crossed the Red Sea. The lessons of the two Judaisms are, of course, not the same. The Judaism of the dual Torah teaches about the sanctification of the everyday in the road toward the salvation of the holy people. The Judaism of Holocaust and Redemption tells me that the everyday—the here and the now of home and family—ends not in a new Eden but in a cloud of gas; that salvation lies today, if I will it, but not here and not now. And it teaches me not only not to trouble to sanctify, but also not even to trust, the present circumstance.

The *Alenu* ("who has not made us like the nations of the world") bears the redeeming message that, in the end, the

[22]

nations of the world will become like us in worshiping the one true God, creator of heaven and earth. The task incumbent on me because of the Judaism of Holocaust and Redemption, its *Alenu,* leads me toward a humanity in the image not of the divine but of the demonic. The great theologian of the Judaism of Holocaust and Redemption Emil Fackenheim has often maintained that the Holocaust produced an eleventh commandment: "Not to hand Hitler any more victories." The commanding voice of Sinai gave Ten Commandments; the commanding voice of Auschwitz, that eleventh. The Ten call for us to become like God in the ways in which the image of God may be graven upon us human beings: that is, by keeping the Sabbath and honoring the other and having no other gods but God. The eleventh tells us what we must not do; it appeals to us not to love God but to spite a man. So does politics transform.

The Judaism of Holocaust and Redemption supplies the words that make another world of this one. Those words, moreover, change the assembly of like-minded individuals into an occasion for the celebration of the group and the commemoration of their shared memories. Not only so, but events defined, meetings called, moments identified as distinctive and holy, by that Judaism of Holocaust and Redemption, mark the public calendar and draw people from home and family to collectivity and community—those events, and, except for specified reasons, not the occasions of the sacred calendar of the synagogue; that is, the life of Israel as defined by the Torah. Just as in the United States religions address the realm of individuals and families but a civil religion—Thanksgiving, the Fourth of July, the rites of politics—defines public discourse on matters of value and ultimate concern, so the Judaism of the dual Torah forms the counterpart to Christianity, and the Judaism of Holocaust and Redemption, as I said, constitutes Jewry's civil religion.

Let me now define in detail this other and competing Judaism, and explain its political program. Only then shall we be able to assess the impact, upon the received Judaism, of the civil religion comprised by Holocaust and Redemption. The "Holocaust" of the Judaism of Holocaust and Redemption refers to the murder of six million Jewish children, women, and men in Europe from 1933 through 1945 by Nazi Germany. The "Redemption" is the creation of the State of Israel. Both events constitute essentially political happenings: a government did the one; a state and government emerged from the other. And both events involved collectivities acting in the realm of public policy. The world view of the Judaism of Holocaust and Redemption stresses the unique character of the murders of European Jews, the providential and redemptive meaning of the creation of the State of Israel. The way of life of the Judaism of Holocaust and Redemption requires active work in raising money and political support for the State of Israel. Different from Zionism, which holds that Jews should live in a Jewish state, this system serves in particular to give Jews living in America a reason and an explanation for being Jewish. This Judaism, therefore, lays particular stress on the complementarity of the political experiences of mid-twentieth-century Jewry: the mass murder in death factories of six million of the Jews of Europe, and the creation of the State of Israel three years after the end of the massacre. These events, together seen as providential, bear the names *holocaust,* for the murders, and *redemption,* for the formation of the State of Israel in the aftermath. The system as a whole presents an encompassing myth, linking one event to the other as an instructive pattern, as I said, and moves Jews to follow a particular set of actions, rather than other sorts, as it tells them why they should be Jewish. In all, the civil religion of Jewry addresses issues of definition of the group and the policies it should follow to sustain its ongoing life and protect its integrity.

The Judaism of Holocaust and Redemption affirms and explains in this-worldly terms the Jews' distinctiveness. It forms, within Jewry, a chapter in a larger movement of ethnic assertion in America. Attaining popularity in the late 1960s, the Judaism of Holocaust and Redemption came to the surface at the same time that black assertion, Italo-American and Polish-American affirmation, and feminism movements for self-esteem without regard to sexual preference attained prominence. That movement of rediscovery of difference responded to the completion of the assimilation to American civilization and its norms. Once people spoke English without a foreign accent, they could think about learning Polish or Yiddish or Norwegian once more. It then became safe and charming. Just as when black students demanded what they deemed ethnically characteristic food, so Jewish students discovered they wanted kosher food, too. In that context, the Judaism of Holocaust and Redemption came into sharp focus, with its answers to unavoidable questions deemed to relate to public policy: Who are we? Why should we be Jewish? What does it mean to be Jewish? How do we relate to Jews in other times and places? What is "Israel," meaning the State of Israel, to us, and what are we to it? Who are we in American society? These and other questions form the agenda for the Judaism of Holocaust and Redemption.

The power of the Judaism of the Holocaust and Redemption to frame Jews' public policy—to the exclusion of the Judaism of the dual Torah—may be shown very simply. The

Holocaust formed the question; Redemption, in the form of the creation of the State of Israel, the answer, for all universal Jewish public activity and discourse. Synagogues except for specified occasions appeal to a few, but activities that express the competing Judaism appeal to nearly everybody. That is to say, nearly all American Jews identify with the State of Israel and regard its welfare as more than a secular good: as a metaphysical necessity, as the other chapter of the Holocaust. Nearly all American Jews are not only supporters of the State of Israel; they also regard their own "being Jewish" as inextricably bound up with the meaning they impute to the Jewish state.* In many ways these Jews every day of their lives relive the terror-filled years in which European Jews were wiped out—*and every day they do something about it.* It is as if people spent their lives trying to live out a cosmic myth, and, through rites of expiation and regeneration, accomplished the goal of purification and renewal. Access to the life of feeling and experience—to the way of life that makes one distinctive without leaving the person terribly different from everybody

---

*I do not mean to suggest that American Judaism constitutes a version of Zionism. Zionism maintains that Jews who do not live in the Jewish state are in exile: there is no escaping that simple allegation, which must call into question that facile affirmation of Zionism central to American Judaism. Zionism further declares that Jews who do not live in the State of Israel must aspire to migrate to that nation or, at the very least, raise their children as potential emigrants: on this position, American Judaism chokes. Zionism holds, moreover, that all Jews must concede— indeed, affirm—the centrality of Jerusalem, and of the State of Israel, in the life of Jews throughout the world. Zionism draws the necessary consequence that Jews who live outside of the State of Israel are in significant ways less "good Jews" than the ones who live there. Now all of these positions, commonplace in Israeli Zionism and certainly accepted—in benign verbal formulations, to be sure—by American Jews, contradict the simple facts of the situation of American Jews and their Judaism. First, they do not think that they are in exile: their Judaism makes no concession on that point. Second, they do not have the remotest thought of emigrating from America to the State of Israel—even though on ceremonial occasions they may not protest when Israelis declare such to be their duty.

else—emerged in the Judaic system of Holocaust and Redemption. The Judaism of Holocaust and Redemption presents an immediately accessible message, cast in extreme emotions of terror and triumph, its round of endless activity demanding only spare time. That Judaism realizes in a poignant way the conflicting demands of Jewish Americans to be intensely Jewish, but only once in a while, and provides a means of expressing difference in public and in politics while not exacting much of a cost in meaningful everyday difference from others.

In addition to the Judaism of the dual Torah, therefore, Jewish North and Latin Americans, West Europeans, Australians and South Africans share a transforming perspective, which imparts to their public, as much as to their private, vision a different set of spectacles from those worn by everybody else in the sheltering society of America or Canada. There is not only a Jewish-ethnic, but a Judaic-religious, corporate experience out there; and, while it self-evidently does not lead to the synagogue, it does enchant vision and change perspective and persons. There are myths and rites to which people respond, even though they are not those of the received Judaism. And, as I shall suggest, the Judaic system that takes the place, in the life of the community at large, of the received Judaism indeed occupies its share of the place reserved for the unique, the self-evident truths beyond argument.

But before proceeding to sort out the two Judaisms and ask how each works its enchantment to transform ordinary people into saints and martyrs, let us turn back to the first of the two, the Judaism of the dual Torah. We want to know where, when, why, and how that Judaism enchants a person and turns that person into something else, something wonderful, more than he or she ever imagined possible: in God's image, after God's likeness. What words do we say, what songs do we sing, to make celestial music? And, more critical still, we want to know what pockets of life we leave open and accessible to paradise. When do we make, and also listen to, that music, and when not? When I know what occasions in here, in my private life, leave me open to the labor of analogy and metaphor that compares me to something else and makes me reach beyond myself, then I know which words enchant what worlds.

PART I
Rites of the Individual

CHAPTER 2

The Grace after Meals: Where We Eat, What We Eat

WHAT HAPPENS in a moment of enchantment is change, not in what we are but in what we perceive. The raw facts of life remain. But, simmered in hot imagination, they form sustaining broth. Take, for instance, a simple meal. I am hungry, I eat, I am satisfied. How commonplace! But if you know, and say, the right words, going from hunger to satisfaction marks a deeper change. You stand for more than you knew, your commonplace meal turns into a remarkable event, and what you thought routine marks the measure of the extraordinary dimension of existence. That is what I mean when I speak of enchantment and transformation: showing the remarkable in the ordinary, changing the routine into the extraordinary. And this wonder can work every time I eat lunch: charmed life indeed! What changes, specifically, three times through the three meals of a day is my notion of where I am eating, of what I am eating, and of the meaning of my eating at all. My sense of what hunger and nourishment, in my private being, stand for is changed. For these mere facts of hunger and satisfaction now represent exile and return, sin and remission of sin, this world and the world to come—all of those complementary opposites that bring to concrete expression that life lived *as if,* that existence as metaphor and simile, that begins in the startling notion that humanity is "in our image, after our likeness." To be a Jew is to live *as if,* to work out the meaning of a metaphor; and three meals a day precipitate the enchantment that, through words, transforms the here and now into something other. Hence, the enchantment of the Grace after Meals (in Hebrew, *Birkat Hammazon*), which transforms my routine experience of hunger and satisfaction into a metaphor for Israel's life of anguished reality but ultimate redemption. So a meal turns into a moment of communion with the meaning of my life as particle of Israel, God's people.

When I was growing up, I knew that Jews said a blessing over bread before meals. In summer camp, the blessing "Blessed are you, Lord our God, king of the world, who brings forth bread from the earth" preceded every meal. (The closing words in Hebrew, *min haarets,* "from the earth," would come out "Minnie Horowitz"; and for a while I wondered, Who is Minnie Horowitz and how come she has her name spoken before every meal?) But I never heard of the Grace after Meals. Now nearly all Jews who attend Jewish public events have encountered the Grace after Meals. The ancient rite began its progress in summer camps and youth groups— among, first, the Orthodox, who of course had never given it up, and the Conservatives. It made its way within the Reform youth movement, and now it is common for the Grace after Meals to be publicly sung in Jewish gatherings everywhere. But the public singing itself marks a shift from the received rite, since, for the Orthodox and some Conservatives, the Grace is said silently and privately, though beginning with a public call to worship; while for the community at large, a vigorous but simple march tune, not in the minor but in the

[32]

major key (when sung right, of C), imposes its martial meaning on the otherworldly words. The music tells me I am in
America, and I might be singing a hymn in a church or a school
song at the end of a football game—or, for that matter, the
national anthem of a banana republic. But the words—listen
to the words, starting with a psalm that varies from weekdays
to Sabbaths and festivals.

On routine weekdays, one psalm prefaces the Grace; and on
Sabbaths and festivals, another psalm is sung. The two—quite
naturally—form a match and a complement. Let us consider
them in sequence. First the psalm for every day:

> By the rivers of Babylon we sat down and wept, when
> we remembered Zion. . . . If I forget you, O Jerusalem, let
> my right hand wither away, let my tongue cling to the roof
> of my mouth if I do not remember you, if I do not set
> Jerusalem above my highest joy. (Psalm 137:1, 5)

Now the psalm for the Sabbath or a festival:

> When the Lord brought back those that returned to
> Zion, we were like dreamers. Our mouth was filled with
> laughter, our tongue with singing. Restore our fortunes, O
> Lord, as the streams in the dry land. They that sow in tears
> shall reap in joy. (Psalm 126:1–2, 4–5)

The contrast tells the story. On weekdays, we are in the here
and now of exile; on the Sabbath or a festival, we refer to the
then and there of Zion as the world of redemption and salvation. The eating of the meal involves more than an individual's
eating food. It involves us—the group—with history and
destiny and invokes the specific moments—time past on week-

days, time future on holy days—that make the group distinctive, with a destiny all its own. So the setting of the meal tells me I am more than who, when I sat down because I was hungry, I thought I was. It identifies the hunger with one historical moment, the satisfaction with another. I was hungry and I ate and had enough. We hungered but were fed and will have enough. From the *I* and the here and now, the occasion of the meal has moved me to the *we* of time and eternity. From the individual's experience of hunger and satiation, I draw inferences about the encounter with calamity and renewal, today and the Sabbath, this life and the coming age. The Psalms chosen as prelude to the Grace after Meals set the scene. Now to the action.

To understand the occasion and the setting, we must recall that in classical Judaism the table at which meals were eaten was regarded as the equivalent of the sacred altar in the Temple.* Judaism taught that each Jew before eating had to attain the same state of ritual purity as the priest in the sacred act of making a sacrifice. So in the classic tradition the Grace after Meals is recited in a sacerdotal circumstance. The Grace is in four principal paragraphs, moving from the here and now to the time to come, from the meal just eaten to the messianic banquet. We start with the ordinary and say what is required: thanks for a real meal in today's world:

Blessed art Thou, Lord our God, King of the Universe, who nourishes all the world by His goodness, in grace, in mercy, and in compassion: He gives bread to all flesh, for His mercy is everlasting. And because of His great goodness

*In chapter 11, the power of that metaphor of prayer for cult in the Temple will recur in yet another way.

we have never lacked, and so may we never lack, sustenance—for the sake of His great Name. For He nourishes
and feeds everyone, is good to all, and provides food for
each one of the creatures He created.

Blessed art Thou, O Lord, who feeds everyone.

The first of the four principal paragraphs leaves us where we
were: at the table at which we ate our meal. It effects no
transformation, for it does not claim that we are someone other
than whom we knew when we began the meal that we were,
and it does not say that we are located somewhere else. More
to the point, the statement does not claim that we have eaten
other than ordinary food, grown anywhere. What it does say
is the unexceptional thought that God has given food, which
any religious person may affirm. The reason is that the food
is not transformed, any more than we are.

Now comes the first unanticipated statement:

We thank Thee, Lord our God, for having given our
fathers as a heritage a pleasant, a good and spacious land; for
having taken us out of the land of Egypt, for having
redeemed us from the house of bondage; for Thy covenant,
which Thou hast set as a seal in our flesh, for Thy Torah
which Thou has taught us, for Thy statutes which Thou hast
made known to us, for the life of grace and mercy Thou
hast graciously bestowed upon us, and for the nourishment
with which Thou dost nourish us and feed us always, every
day, in every season, and every hour.

For all these things, Lord our God, we thank and praise
Thee; may Thy praises continually be in the mouth of every
living thing, as it is written, *And thou shalt eat and be satisfied,*

and bless the Lord thy God for the good land which He hath given thee.

Blessed art Thou, O Lord, for the land and its food.

We have moved from what we have eaten to where we have eaten. But that introduces a dissonant note: Where am I, and who am I? I am no longer merely someone who has eaten a meal. My thanks go for more than the food. Now I refer to a "good and spacious land," meaning only what Judaism knows as the Land of Israel; to "us," not me; to "our fathers"; to having been taken "out of the land of Egypt," having been redeemed from slavery; to a covenant in "our flesh"; to Torah and statutes; and on and on, down to land and food.

A considerable realm of being has taken over everyday reality. I am no longer what I thought: a hungry man who has eaten lunch. Now, on the occasion of a cheese sandwich, I invoke the entire sacred history of Israel, the Jewish people, from the Exodus from Egypt to the circumcision of my penis. All invoked for a single occasion, a meal that has changed my condition from one of hunger to one of satisfaction. And that is the very meaning of the transformation, through the enchantment of the statements at hand, of every meal—or, for the generality of Jews, many public and communal meals—into the re-enactment of the former and present condition of Israel, the holy people.

Not only so, but the occasion points toward the end as well:

O Lord our God, have pity on Thy people Israel, on Thy city Jerusalem, on Zion the place of Thy glory, on the royal house of David Thy Messiah, and on the great and holy house which is called by Thy Name. Our God, our Father, feed us and speed us, nourish us and make us flourish, unstintingly, O Lord our God, speedily free us from all distress.

And let us not, O Lord our God, find ourselves in need of gifts from flesh and blood, or of a loan from anyone save from Thy full, generous, abundant, wide-open hand; so we may never be humiliated, or put to shame.

O rebuild Jerusalem, the holy city, speedily in our day. Blessed art Thou, Lord, who in mercy will rebuild Jerusalem. Amen.

The climax refers to Jerusalem, Zion, David, the Messiah, the Temple—where God was sustained in times past; then to dependence on God alone, not on mortals; and to the rebuilding of Jerusalem. All of these closely related symbols invoke the single consideration of time at its end: the coming of the Messiah and the conclusion of history as we now know it. The opening Psalms have prepared us for this appeal to the end-time: exile on weekdays, return to Zion on Sabbaths and holy days.

The fourth paragraph of the Grace after Meals returns us to the point where we began—thanks for lunch:

Blessed art Thou, Lord our God, King of the Universe, Thou God, who art our Father, our powerful king, our creator and redeemer, who made us, our holy one, the holy one of Jacob, our shepherd, shepherd of Israel, the good king, who visits His goodness upon all; for every single day He has brought good, He does bring good, He will bring good upon us; He has rewarded us, does regard, and will always reward us, with grace, mercy and compassion, amplitude, deliverance and prosperity, blessing and salvation, comfort, and a living, sustenance, pity and peace, and all good—let us not want any manner of good whatever.

Of the four paragraphs of the Grace after Meals, the first and the fourth, which multiply prayers for future grace alongside thanks for goodness now received, begin and end in the here and now. The two in the middle invoke a different being altogether.

I have eaten an ordinary meal in the here and now. I invoke the entire history of Israel, refer to the holy land and food produced there, and so transform a cheese sandwich into a foretaste of eternity in the land of God's choosing for me. I eat anywhere, nowhere in particular, but am located by the sacred words in some one place. Eating is turned paradoxically into a locative experience, identifying my right place with somewhere else than where I now am. Where I eat has no bearing, any more than has what I eat, on what has really happened. For I was hungry and now am satisfied; and in that experience, in my very natural and fleshly body, I have lived out the life of time and eternity. The transformation of the ordinary into the unusual effected by the rehearsal of holy land and sacred history moves present time and perceived space from now to then, then past, then future. In seeing matters in this way, Judaism perceives things as other than they are. And that mode of thought, we shall see time and again, characterizes the Judaic experience of the everyday.

That power of vision to turn reality into something else, which we see in the force of words to change a meal, rewrites Israel's history as well, placing at the center of that history the relationship of the holy people to the holy land. Israel's history, in a this-worldly sense, consisted of the secular affairs of a seldom important kingdom, able to hold its own only when its neighbors permitted or could not prevent it. In the mythic context, however, Jews looked back upon the land as not a given but a gift, and upon the history of the people as a continuing revelation of divine justice and mercy. Israel, the people, kept the Torah; therefore, they enjoyed peace and prospered. Then Israel sinned, so God called forth instruments of His wrath: Philistines, Assyrians, Babylonians, Persians, Greeks, Romans—there was no end to the list as time went on. But when Israel was properly chastised, God restored its people's prosperity and brought them back to the land. The land therefore stood for much else; holding the land or losing it marked the engagement of God with the people. No wonder, then, that at every meal (for some) or at important public occasions of rehearsal and renewal (for many), the eating of a meal should precipitate the transformation of individuals into a group, thanking God as a *we,* as Israel, not only for the food just now consumed—the produce of Ohio or California—but for the nourishment of the land.

Perhaps the single most powerful worldly experience in the history of Judaism was the destruction of the First Temple in 586 B.C.E., followed by the restoration of Jews to their land by the Persians approximately a half-century later. The worldly motives of the Persians are of no interest here, for they never played a role in the interpretation of historical events put forward by Judaic tradition. What the Jews understood was simply this: God had punished them, but when they repented and atoned, He had forgiven and redeemed them. And they further believed that the prophets who had foretold just this pattern of events were now vindicated, so that much else that the prophets said was likely to be true. From the fifth century before the Common Era to the present, Jews have seen their history—which is to say, their theology—within the paradigm of sin, punishment, atonement, reconciliation, and then restoration.

The land entered the Judaic imagination as a powerful—indeed, overwhelming—symbol. It was holy, the state for sacred history. I have already noted numerous references to the land, Jerusalem, Zion, and the like—references that all are concrete exemplifications of myth. Redemption is not an abstract concept, but rather is what happened when Moses led the people through the Sea of Reeds, or what happened with the return to Zion when the Second Temple was built (*c.* 500 B.C.E.), or what will happen when God again shines light on Zion and brings the scattered people back to their homes. In classical Judaism, the sanctity of the land, the yearning for Zion, the hope for the restoration of Jerusalem and the Temple cult are all symbols by which the redemption of the past is projected on to the future. The equivalent of the salvation at the sea will be the restoration of Israel to the land and the reconstruction of the Temple and of Jerusalem: the one stands at the beginning of Israel's history; the other, its counterpart, at the end.

The context of grace is enjoyment of creation, through which God nourishes the world in His goodness. That we have had this meal—however humble—is not to be taken for granted, but rather to be accepted as a gift, just as the land is a gift. Whenever one eats, he or she must reflect on the beneficence of the Creator. The arena for creation is the land, which to the ordinary eye is commonplace, small, dry, rocky; but which to the eye of faith is pleasant, good, spacious. The land lay at the end of redemption from Egyptian bondage. Holding it, enjoying it—as we shall see, in chapter 11, in the *Shema*—is a sign that the covenant is intact and in force, and that Israel is loyal to its part of the contract and God to His.

Grace after Meals: Where We Eat, What We Eat

The land, the Exodus, the covenant—these all depend upon the Torah, the statutes, and a life of grace and mercy, here embodied in and evoked by the nourishment of the meal. Thanksgiving wells up, and the paragraph ends with praises for the land and its food. Then the chief theme recurs—that is, redemption and hope for return, and then future prosperity in the land: "May God pity the people, the city, Zion, the royal house of the Messiah, the Holy Temple." The nourishment of this meal is but a foretaste of the nourishment of the messianic time, just as the joy of the wedding is a foretaste of the messianic rejoicing. Still, it is not the messianic time, so Israel finally asks not to depend upon the gifts of mortal men but only upon those of the generous, wide-open hand of God. And then "rebuild Jerusalem." The concluding paragraph summarizes the whole, giving thanks for creation, redemption, divine goodness, every blessing.

To conclude: What has happened at the meal is simple. The diner was hungry and ate—a commonplace, entirely secular action. But the experience of hunger and of eating is turned, through the medium of words, into an encounter with another world of meaning altogether. The rite, an act of thought and imagination, transforms time and space, moving us from nowhere in particular to a particular place, changing me and all of us from the here and the now into the social entity of the past and the future then. The words we say change the world of the *I* by telling me I am more than in the here and now and live more than in the perceived present, because I am more than a mere *I* but part of a larger *we*—all because of words I say when I eat lunch. What greater enchantment than that!

Hunger, meal, satisfaction—these invoke one encounter with enchantment. Another hunger, another fulfillment, involves the hunger to live beyond our own lifetime, the urge and need for sexual love, then the satisfaction of the hunger and the need in the birth of a child. That common human experience is transformed through the enchantment of the rite of *berit milah,* the covenant with God effected through circumcision, which, like Grace after Meals, leads us from our this-worldly human experience to an otherworldly reading of that experience. This life once more becomes a metaphor for another, and we live *as if:* in an image, after a likeness. The enchantment lies in our understanding that we are the image, we are the likeness. Beyond lies that which we reflect, that reality to which we are likened. Through our imagination we perceive reality: we are the metaphor; therefore, even our simple meal invokes comparison, wherein a magic dwells.

CHAPTER 3

The Rite of Circumcision: The "Others" Who Come to Celebrate

THE BIRTH of a child, unlike the meal that moves us from hunger to satisfaction, is unique. But both experiences, hardly congruent in intensity, are the same in sentiment, attitude, and emotion. We go from hunger—whether for food or immortality through at least another generation—to satisfaction, from not having to having the perquisite of life. What we say and do may treat the moment as metaphor of the radical turning in life, or leave the occasion unchanged. The words of enchantment in the case of Judaism transform the birth of the child from a private and personal happening in the natural family to a public and momentous event in the life of the supernatural family of Israel on earth and of God in heaven. That rite of enchantment frames a deed and the words said at its doing, and in attendance are not only family and friends of the here and now but one who was present at the original deed. Specifically, in the case of a boy child, a minor surgical rite, of dubious medical value, becomes the mark of the renewal of the agreement between God and Israel, the covenant carved into the flesh of the penis of every Jewish male—and nothing less. The beginning of a new life renews the rule that governs Israel's relationship to God. So the private joy is reworked through words of enchantment—once more, sanctification— and so transformed into renewal of the community of Israel and God.

Once more, we are not only in the here and now: we are in another time, another place. We do not only what we do—the cutting of the flesh, the manipulation of the blood, the drinking of wine; we translate the deeds into other dimensions altogether. And at issue, above all, is not the *I* but the *we,* the transformation radical beyond all other changes.

The rite of passage of circumcision in Judaism involves, therefore, a most personal moment, the birth of a child because of the private sexual relation of the mother and the father and the personal travail of the mother. That most individual occasion, the beginning of a person's life, links in a concrete way to specific moments and personalities in the public and supernatural life of Israel. On a Jewish son is performed a surgical operation in the name of the faith, by cutting off the foreskin of the penis and calling the rite *berit milah:* the covenant *(berit)* effected through the rite of circumcision *(milah). Berit milah* seals with the blood of the infant son the contract between Israel and God, generation by generation, son by son.

Circumcision must take place on the eighth day after birth, normally in the presence of a quorum of ten adult males. Commonly, it is done in the home, not in the hospital; and crowded into a few rooms will be relatives and friends. There is nothing private or merely surgical about the operation. The contemporary practice of having a surgical operation in no way carries out the rite of circumcision. For what changes the matter is not only circumstance. It is the formula, the words of blessing that form the counterpart to the Grace after Meals, the medium of enchantment that transforms the birth of a child to an individual couple into an event heavy with meaning: a metaphor for something more, for something that transcends.

But that deep significance is psychologically quite natural. For no moment in the passage of life from birth to death so touches a parent as does the birth of a child. Questions of past and future weigh heavily on the present. The parent looks backward, toward family perhaps for a time—as young people find expedient—neglected, and directs hopes forward, toward a future of perfection to be realized by the child, a perfection unattained by the parents themselves and likely unattainable by any mortal: so great is the power of dreaming. Fathers and mothers now become grandparents; siblings, uncles and aunts: a new social entity takes shape around the new person. When, on such an occasion, Judaism intervenes, exhausted mother and happy, confused father will do pretty much whatever they are told in the name of a blessing for the child—if only *"Mazal tov"* (meaning "under a good star").

When my second son, Eli, was to be circumcised, in Hanover, New Hampshire, the presiding *mohel*—the specialist in the rite of circumcision whom we had imported from faraway Lawrence, Massachusetts—instructed my father-in-law, who was holding the child, to sit on our dining room table. The *mohel* had in mind the necessity of the child's being held at a height convenient for the rite. What my father-in-law had in mind I do not know. He simply sat where he was told—square on the center of our dining-room table. The table collapsed. The baby bounced on the floor (surviving nicely, he grew up—to my horror!—to be a varsity rugby player on Columbia's starting team). I retreated. Happily, others sterilized and reset the instruments, and the rite went forward. When later, after all had ended well, I asked my father-in-law why he had sat on the table, he said, "The *mohel* told me to. I thought it was part of the rite." I said, "And had he told you to wash the baby in seaweed, would you have done that, too?" And he said, "You would have, why shouldn't I?" And he was right.

Enchantment works in a mysterious way to make us do things we should not ordinarily do, to see things we commonly do not perceive. But in the case of Judaism, the words make sense, evoking in the intimacy of the private life the being that we share together: Israel, its covenant with God, its origin in Abraham, Isaac, Jacob. We see ourselves as—in the setting of Judaism—God sees us: a family beyond time, joined by blood of not pedigree but circumcision; a genealogy framed by fifty generations of loyalty to the covenant in blood; and a birth from the union of the womb of a Jewish woman with the circumcised penis of her husband. This is the fruit of the womb—my son, my son, my son.

There are four aspects in which the operation is turned into a rite. When the rite begins, the assembly and the *mohel* together recite the following:

> The Lord spoke to Moses saying, Phineas, son of Eleazar, son of Aaron, the priest, has turned my wrath from the Israelites by displaying among them his passion for me, so that I did not wipe out the Israelite people in my passion. Say therefore I grant him my covenant of peace.

Commenting on this passage, Lifsa Schachter states, "Phineas is identified with zealously opposing the . . . sins of sexual licentiousness and idolatry. He is best known for an event which occurred when the Israelites, whoring with Moabite

women in the desert, were drawn to the worship of Baal-Peor.
. . . Phineas leaped into the fray and through an act of double
murder . . . quieted God's terrible wrath."[1]

Second, in looking around the room where the rite takes
place, we notice that a chair is set called the "chair of Elijah":
thus, the rite takes place in the presence of a chair for Elijah,
the prophet. The newborn son is set on that chair, and the
congregation says, "This is the chair of Elijah, of blessed
memory." Elijah, having complained to God that Israel neglected the covenant (I Kings 19:10–14), he comes to bear
witness that Israel observes the covenant of circumcision.
Then, before the surgical operation, a blessing is said. Third,
after the operation, a blessing is said over a cup of wine.

Let me take up each of these matters and explore their
meaning. To understand the invocation of Elijah, for whom
we set a chair (and whom we shall meet again at the Passover
seder), we first recall the pertinent biblical passage:

> Suddenly the word of the Lord came to him: "Why are
> you here, Elijah?"
> "Because of my great zeal for the Lord the God of hosts,"
> he said. "The people of Israel have forsaken your covenant,
> torn down your altars, and put your prophets to death with
> the sword. I alone am left, and they seek to take my life."
> The answer came: "Go and stand on the mount before
> the Lord."
> For the Lord was passing by: a great and strong wind
> came rending mountains and shattering rocks before him,
> but the Lord was not in the wind; and after the wind there
> was an earthquake, but the Lord was not in the earthquake;
> and after the earthquake fire; but the Lord was not in the
> fire; and after the fire a still small voice.

When Elijah heard it, he muffled his face in his cloak and went out and stood at the entrance of the cave. Then there came a voice: "Why are you here, Elijah?"

"Because of my great zeal for the Lord God of hosts," he said. "The people of Israel have forsaken your covenant, torn down your altars, and put your prophets to death with the sword. I alone am left, and they seek to take my life."

(I Kings 19:10–14)

This passage stands behind the story told in a medieval document, *Pirke deRabbi Eliezer,* that Elijah attends the rite of circumcision of every Jewish baby boy:

The Israelites were wont to circumcise until they were divided into two kingdoms. The kingdom of Ephraim cast off from themselves the covenant of circumcision. Elijah, may he be remembered for good, arose and was zealous with a mighty passion, and he adjured the heavens to send down neither dew nor rain upon the earth. Jezebel heard about it and sought to slay him.

Elijah arose and prayed before the Holy One, blessed be he. The Holy One, blessed be he, said to him, *"Are you better than your fathers* [I Kings 19:4]? Esau sought to slay Jacob, but he fled before him, as it is said, *And Jacob fled into the field of Aram* [Hosea 12:12].

"Pharaoh sought to slay Moses, who fled before him and he was saved, as it is said, *Now when Pharaoh heard this thing, he sought to slay Moses. And Moses fled from the face of Pharaoh* [Ezekiel 2:15].

"Saul sought to slay David, who fled before him and was

[48]

saved, as it is said, *If you save not your life tonight, tomorrow you will be killed* [1 Samuel 19:11]."

Another text says, *And David fled and escaped* [1 Samuel 19:18]. Learn that everyone who flees is sad.

Elijah, may he be remembered for good, arose and fled from the land of Israel, and he betook himself to Mount Horeb, as it is said, *and he arose and ate and drank* [1 Kings 19:8].

Then the Holy One, blessed be he, was revealed to him and said to him, "What are you doing here, Elijah?"

He answered him saying, "I have been very zealous."

The Holy One, blessed be he, said to him, "You are always zealous. You were zealous in Shittim on account of the immortality. For it is said, *Phineas, the son of Eleazar, the son of Aaron the priest, turned my wrath away from the children of Israel, in that he was zealous with my zeal among them* [Numbers 25:11].

"Here you are also zealous, By your life! They shall not observe the covenant of circumcision until you see it done with your own eyes."

Hence the sages have instituted the custom that people should have a seat of honor for the messenger of the covenant, for Elijah, may he be remembered for good, is called the messenger of the covenant, as it is said, *And the messenger of the covenant, whom you delight in, behold he comes* [Malachi 3:1].[2]

So, too, the "messenger of the covenant" is the prophet Elijah, and he is present whenever a Jewish son enters the *covenant* of Abraham, which is circumcision. God ordered Elijah to come to every circumcision so as to witness the loyalty of the Jews to the covenant. Elijah, then, serves as the guardian for the newborn, just as he raised the child of the widow from the dead (1 Kings 17:17–24). Along these same lines, as we shall see on the *seder* table of Passover, a cup of wine is poured for Elijah, and the door is opened for Elijah to join in the rite. Setting a seat for Elijah serves to invoke the presence of the guardian of the newborn and the zealous advocate of the rite of the circumcision of the covenant. Thus, celebrating with the family of the newborn are not "all Israel" in general, but a specific personage indeed. The gesture of setting the chair silently sets the stage for an event in the life of the family not of the child alone but of all Israel. The chair of Elijah, filled by the one who holds the child, sets the newborn baby into Elijah's lap. The enchantment extends through the furnishing of the room; what is not ordinarily present is introduced, and that makes all the difference.

We move, third, from gesture to formula, for a blessing is said after the rite itself: that is, the *mohel* takes the knife and cuts the foreskin, and then these words are said by the father:

> Praised are You . . . who sanctified us with Your commandments and commanded us to bring the son into the covenant of Abraham our father.

The explicit invocation of Abraham's covenant turns the concrete action in the here and now into a simile of the paradigm and archetype: I circumcise my son just as Abraham circumcised Isaac at eight days, and Ishmael. What I do is like what Abraham did. Things are more than what they seem. Then I am a father, like Abraham, and—more to the point—my fatherhood is like Abraham's.

The operation done, the wine is blessed, introducing yet a further occasion of enchantment:

The Rite of Circumcision

Praised are You, Lord our God, who sanctified the beloved from the womb and set a statute into his very flesh, and his parts sealed with the sign of the holy covenant. On this account, Living God, our portion and rock, save the beloved of our flesh from destruction, for the sake of his covenant placed in our flesh. Blessed are You . . . who makes the covenant.

The covenant is not a generality; it is specific, concrete, fleshly. It is, moreover, meant to accomplish a specific goal—as all religion means to attain concrete purposes—and that is to secure a place for the child, a blessing for the child. By virtue of the rite, the child enters the covenant: he joins that unseen "Israel" that through blood enters an agreement with God. Then the blessing of the covenant is owing to the child. For covenants or contracts cut both ways.

After the father has recited the blessing—". . . who has sanctified us by his commandments and has commanded us to induct him into the covenant of our father, Abraham"—the community of ten males responds: "Just as he has entered the covenant, so may he be introduced to Torah, the *huppah* [marriage canopy] and good deeds."

Schachter interprets those "others" who are present as follows:

In the presence of Elijah . . . *Torah*—as against idolatry; in the presence of Phineas . . . *huppah,* as against sexual licentiousness; in the presence of Abraham . . . to *good deeds: For I have singled him out that he may instruct his children and his posterity to keep the way of the Lord by doing what is just and right.* [Genesis 18:18][3]

When we speak, following Israel Scheffler, of how rite accomplishes the cognitive ordering of the categories of time, space, action and community, we see how, in Judaism, through a rite of enchantment, in the transformation of the *now* of the birth of the son into the *then* of Abraham's covenant with God, people make a public event of a private joy. And this constitutes a statement, not merely an expression of feeling. There is, in what is said, both a voice and an echo. The voice speaks clearly; the words evoke the scene: Elijah complaining to God; Abraham obediently circumcising his sons; Phineas calming God's wrath by an act of violence, with whom a covenant of peace then is made. Though the echo is muffled, we hear the gist of the message: what we do we do together and in public.

There is not only an *I,* there is a *we,* and each of us is always *we.* That I take to be what is transformed through the enchantment of the blessing prior to the act and the blessing over the cup of wine. I am no longer in the here and the now; time is other than what I thought. I am no longer in my dining room. Space is revised: a chair is set, a rite takes place. The action is not the cutting of the flesh but the covenant of circumcision. And present are my wife and my father-in-law and my baby son on the floor, surrounded by knives and gauze. Present here, too, is the statement that we are Israel—yet, in the here and now, the dazed father; the bemused, enchanted grandfather; the sturdy son. Varsity rugby for Columbia indeed!

CHAPTER 4

The Marriage Ceremony: *You* and *I* Become Adam and Eve

NO GREATER JOY marks life than the beginning of a marriage, moment of perfect illusion. The bride plans to change the groom; the groom hopes the bride will never change: grand illusion. We say words that legitimate what aforetime was not. That change in a this-worldly sense is merely legal, a change in personal status and consequent property rights and obligations. But, in the enchantment of Judaism, the words transform not only the relationship in law but also the participants (in our Western context) in love. In this way, as in the imaginative rereading of birth of a boy baby, the *we* of you and me becomes the *us* of the social entity. But what *us* and which entity?

Entry into the imaginative world created by the rite of marriage is made easy by the human condition. For, just as the Grace after Meals turns a natural and common experience into the enactment and celebration of another place and time and world altogether, so does the rite of the *huppah* turn something into something else. The words said after a meal affect the personal and merely physical, while those that change the public union of two private persons call upon encompassing eternity. Yet, in the case of the Grace, it is from hunger to satisfaction, from exile to redemption; and in the case of the wedding, it is from the here and the now to Eden past and Zion redeemed at the end of time—perfection to perfection. Still, the experience that all of us have, now changed into a metaphor for something other, is different from the transformation of hunger and satisfaction into the paradigm of the human condition of Israel's suffering and solace.

If my own memory serves for others, then what one goes through as one approaches and enters marriage is the wonderful sense that "This cannot be happening to me." Through the entire process of courtship and marriage I felt like a bystander, unable to cope, as with something real and immediate, with the reality that I was getting married. I could not believe my good fortune—and never afterward took it for granted. The only one I ever wanted said yes. But it was really happening to me, beyond all imagining. I never really hoped, I never really dreamed—yet there I was. No wonder, then, that it seemed like a wonder—and still does. In this moment in which, so it seems, I witness as a bystander what in fact changes me and my life, imagining that I am someone else and somewhere else is not so hard. But who and where?

The enchantment transforms the space, the time, the action, and the community of the *I* of the groom and the *I* of the bride. The space is contained by the *huppah,* translated as "marriage canopy" or "bower," which (rightly done) is constructed under the open sky: a contained space of heaven representing heaven. The time? It is now in the beginning. When else could it be? The action, then, invokes creation, the making of a new Eden. The community of the two *I*'s becom-

ing one *we* is the couple changed into the paradigm of humanity, beginning with Adam and Eve. Stripped down to essen-
tials, the union of woman and man becomes the beginning of
a new creation, the woman becoming Eve; the man, Adam. In
this way is realized the prophecy of the snake in Eden, as
explained by the great medieval Bible interpreter Rashi
(1040–1105). When the snake says, *"But God knows that as soon
as you eat of it, your eyes will be opened and you will be like God"*
(Genesis 3:5), the meaning, according to Rashi, is that you will
become "creators of worlds." At the marriage rite a new world
begins: a family, a social entity, humanity at the beginning of
new creation of life.

That human experience of otherness, of being a bystander
at a great event, is, in my memory, what turns the mere
participant into an actor: someone who is two persons, the self
and the self made other. I dress in costume, not in everyday
clothes. I come in procession; I do not merely walk. I stand
center-stage, the cast well arrayed around me, and well di-
rected. It is natural and right, therefore, that even as I see
myself as a witness to what is, in fact, happening to me as to
an actor in a play, so I should imagine the role I play. A great
actor sees himself as separate from a role even while playing
it: for him, coming into a room is an act he has reflected upon.
That duality of consciousness claims as well the man and the
woman about to marry, and opens up for them the imagination.

Thus, enchantment may change the natural moment into
that something more that, in Judaism, we call holy. If we turn
to the change of place effected by the setting, the marriage
bower, we then ask: Who am I now? And who is she, whom
I marry, in this odd drama in which I see myself as both an
actor playing a role but also as my natural self? The specific

words of enchantment answer that question, and there are two roles combined into one, two stages that blend. The first is the human being representing all humanity: man standing for Adam, who is Man; woman for Eve, that is, Life and Woman. The second role, of course, is the humanity of Israel, the separate and sacred social entity, man and woman standing—through their joy on this unreservedly happy occasion—for Israel's joy but also, therefore, for Israel's sorrow now and redemption then.

The enchantment works not one but many changes in the new stage that is the marriage canopy, for each actor wears two masks, plays two parts—and maybe more. That map of many layers of translucent paper, each with its marking, shows the contours of the way only when all the sheets are in place. In the changed place and altered circumstance of the *I* and *you* become Adam and Eve in Eden, but also rejoicing Israel in the land redeemed, time overflows the boundaries not only of the here and now but of many thens; space is in more than one dimension; the action—as we shall see—is multiple; and the community is not only *you* and *I,* the *we* that takes shape, but that *we* that is all Israel, present at the beginning when an Israel takes place.

That is what it means to say that the most intimate occasion, whether the birth of a child or the marriage ceremony, is also by its nature social, therefore public, communal, historical in a mythic sense. Here a new family begins. Individual lover and beloved celebrate the uniqueness, the privacy of their love. The nuptial prayer cannot, therefore, speak only of him and her, natural man and natural woman, as though the private life alone were celebrated, as if we come from nowhere and go nowhere and make no difference to anyone. The opposite is the truth. I come from a father and a mother, and I become a parent; my life is with people; whatever I am and do is with people, that entity, Israel, conjured by Judaism out of a mass of individuals.

The rite comes to a climax in the Seven Blessings. But it unfolds in stages, beginning before the couple reaches the marriage canopy, ending long afterward. Seen in sequence, the rite follows this pattern: (1) the *ketubah* is witnessed; (2) the bride's veil is put in place by the groom; (3) under the *huppah, erusin;* (4) under the *huppah, nissuin.* If we walk through the rite, stopping at its principal stages, we come first to the touching moment when the groom places the veil over the bride's face, prior to entering under the marriage canopy, and makes the following statement to her:

> May you, our sister, be fruitful and prosper. May God make you as Sarah, Rebecca, Rachel, and Leah. May the Lord bless you and keep you. May the Lord show you favor and be gracious to you. May the Lord show you kindness and grant you peace.[1]

The blessing of the groom for the bride invokes the matriarchs of Israel—a detail we need not find surprising. Rachel makes her appearance in the Seven Blessings; and as soon as we speak of Abraham, we think of Sarah; so, too, Isaac and Rebecca, Jacob and Leah and Rachel.

In focusing upon the drama, we should not lose sight of the occasion. The wedding takes place in the here and now; and in Judaism, we do not lose sight of practical considerations. The bride is not only Eve, she is also a woman who bears responsibility to her husband; and the groom, Adam, is also going to go back to work next week. The task of rite is not only to transform, but also to underline, reality. In the case of

[57]

the *huppah,* the rite of marriage, a legal transaction goes forward, the formation of a social entity, a family, in which the rights and obligations of each party have to reach the expression and guarantee of a contract. In the case of the marriage ceremony, a marriage contract, a *ketubah,* is appropriately signed and delivered from the groom to the bride's possession, and is the first stage in the process. A précis of the *ketubah* follows:

> This ketubah witnesses before God and man that on the —— day of the week, the —— of the month ——, in the year 57—, the holy covenant of marriage was entered between bridgroom and his bride, at——. Duly conscious of the solemn obligation of marriage the bridegroom made the following declaration to his bride: "Be consecrated to me as my wife according to the laws and traditions of Moses and Israel. I will love, honor and cherish you; I will protect and support you; and I will faithfully care for your needs, as prescribed by Jewish law and tradition." And the bride made the following declaration to the groom: "In accepting the wedding ring I pledge you all my love and devotion and I take upon myself the fulfillment of all the duties incumbent upon a Jewish wife."

The Aramaic language of the *ketubah* specifies the legal standing of the husband's obligation to the wife. In order to pay what is owing to her should he divorce her, or in order to provide for her if he dies before she does, the husband pledges even the shirt on his back. No one is playing games.

To understand the next stage in the rite—between the signing of witnesses on the *ketubah* and the recitation of the Seven Blessings—we have to call to mind the law of Judaism.

That law knows a two-stage process: one called *erusin;* the other, *nissuin.* We may roughly represent these stages as betrothal, then marriage. The union of a couple takes place in two stages: *erusin,* in which the woman is sanctified, or designated as holy, to a particular man; and *nissuin,* in which the actual union is consecrated through the Seven Blessings. In ancient times, these stages took place in an interval of as much as a full year, with the rite of designation separated from the consummation by twelve months. But, in our own day, the wedding rite encompasses both.

Erusin is carried out under the marriage canopy as bride and groom drink of a cup of wine and say this blessing:

> Blessed are you, our God, king of the world, who creates the fruit of the vine.
> Blessed are you, Lord our God, king of the world, who has sanctified us by his commandments and commanded us concerning proper sexual relations, forbidding to us betrothed women but permitting to us married women through the rites of the huppah and sanctification. Blessed are you, Lord, who sanctifies his people Israel through the marriage canopy and the rite of sanctification.

Then the bridegroom gives a ring to the bride, with this formula:

> Behold you are sanctified to me by this ring in accord with the tradition of Moses and Israel.

That concludes the chapter of the rite known as *erusin,* which we may translate, with less than exact accuracy, as betrothal.

Then come the Seven Blessings. The climax of the rite of

Adam and Eve, of you and me as Israel in Jerusalem beyond time, comes in the recitation of Seven Blessings *(sheva berakhot)* over a cup of wine. Here is the first of those seven transforming statements of sanctification, which the rabbi or the cantor says over a cup of wine:

> Praised are You, O Lord our God, King of the universe, Creator of the fruit of the vine.

The rite takes its place over the cup of wine; the enchantment begins by turning the wine into something else than what it has been.

Then comes the first action, invoking through words the world of Eden:

> Praised are You, O Lord our God, King of the universe, who created all things for Your glory.
>
> Praised are You, O Lord our God, King of the universe, Creator of Adam.
>
> Praised are You, O Lord our God, King of the universe, who created man and woman in his image, fashioning woman from man as his mate, that together they might perpetuate life. Praised are You, O Lord, Creator of man.

In the second, third, and fourth blessings, the sequence of three is perfectly realized; first, creation of all things; then, creation of Man; then creation of man and woman in God's image. These words invoke a world for which the occasion at hand serves as metaphor. "We now are like them then"—this is what is at stake.

Israel's history begins with creation—first, the creation of the vine, symbol of the natural world. Creation is for God's

[60]

glory. All things speak to nature, to the physical as much as the spiritual, for all things were made by God. In Hebrew, the third blessing ends, "who formed the *Adam.*" All things glorify God; above all creation is Adam. The theme of ancient paradise is introduced by the simple choice of the word *Adam,* heavy with meaning. The myth of Man's creation is rehearsed: Man and Woman are in God's image, together complete and whole, creators of life, "like God." Woman was fashioned from Man together with him to perpetuate life. And, again, "blessed is the creator of Adam." We have moved, therefore, from the natural world to the archetypical realm of paradise. Before us we see not merely a man and a woman, but Adam and Eve.

The enchantment works its wonder by identifying the moment at hand, by telling us what we are like—that is, what is really happening. And under the circumstances formed by that mode of metaphorical thought, the reality that generates meaning is the *out there* of "man and woman in His image," Eden, creation. The *in here*—bride and groom wondering whether this is really true—then matches the *out there.* The world is truly stage; the men and women, truly players. But here, in the fifth blessing, one actor takes two roles at once:

> May Zion rejoice as her children are restored to her in joy. Praised are You, O Lord, who causes Zion to rejoice at her children's return.

A jarring intrusion: Zion comes uninvited. No one mentioned her. But, as we saw in the Grace after Meals *("If I forget you, O Jerusalem")* and given the standing of Zion as metaphor simultaneously for the resolution of Israel's exile and the human condition of suffering, who can find surprising the entry of this new character, this persona?

This Adam and this Eve also are Israel, children of Zion the mother, as expressed in the fifth blessing. Zion lies in ruins, her children scattered. Adam and Eve cannot celebrate together without thought to the condition of the mother, Jerusalem. The children will one day come home. The mood is hopeful yet sad, as it was meant to be, for archaic Israel mourns as it rejoices and rejoices as it mourns. Quickly then, back to the happy occasion, for we do not let mourning lead to melancholy. "Grant perfect joy to the loving companions," for they are creators of a new line in mankind—the new Adam, the new Eve—and of their home: May it be the garden of Eden. And if joy is there, then "praised are you for the joy of bride and groom."

The joy of the moment gives a foretaste of the rejoy of restoration, redemption, return. Now the two roles become one in that same joy: first Adam and Eve, groom and bride; Eden then, the marriage canopy now:

> Grant perfect joy to these loving companions, as You did to the first man and woman in the Garden of Eden. Praised are You, O Lord, who grants the joy of bride and groom.

That same joy comes in the metaphors of Zion the bride and Israel the groom.

In the seventh blessing, the joy is not in two but in three masks: Eden then; marriage party now; and Zion in the coming age:

> Praised are You, O Lord our God, King of the universe, who created joy and gladness, bride and groom, mirth, song, delight and rejoicing, love and harmony, peace and companionship. O Lord our God, may there ever *be heard in the*

*cities of Judah and in the streets of Jerusalem voices of joy and
gladness, voices of bride and groom, the jubilant voices of those
joined in marriage under the bridal canopy, the voices of young
people feasting and singing.*

Here the words in italics allude to the vision of Jeremiah, when
all seemed lost, that Jerusalem, about to fall and lose its people,
will one day ring with the shouts not of the slaughtered and
the enslaved but of the returned and the redeemed. Hence, this
concluding blessing returns to the theme of Jerusalem, evoking
the tragic hour of Jerusalem's first destruction. When everyone
had given up hope, supposing with the end of Jerusalem had
come the end of time, only Jeremiah counseled renewed hope.
With the enemy at the gate, he sang of coming gladness:

Thus says the Lord:
In this place of which you say, "It is a waste, without
man or beast," in the cities of Judah and the streets of
Jerusalem that are desolate, without man or inhabitant or
beast,
There shall be heard again the voice of mirth and the
voice of gladness, the voice of the bridegroom and the voice
of the bride, the voice of those who sing as they bring
thank-offerings to the house of the Lord. . . .
For I shall restore the fortunes of the land as at first, says
the Lord.

(Jeremiah 33:10–11)

The closing blessing is not merely a literary artifice or a
learned allusion to the ancient prophet. It defines the exultant,
jubilant climax of this acted-out myth: Just as here and now
there stand before us Adam and Eve, so here and now in this

wedding, the olden sorrow having been rehearsed, we listen to the voice of gladness that is coming. The joy of this new creation prefigures the joy of the Messiah's coming, hope for which is very present in this hour. And when he comes, the joy then will echo the joy of bride and groom before us. Zion the bride, Israel the groom, united now as they will be reunited by the compassionate God—these stand under the marriage canopy.

But enchantment is just that. In the end, we are who we are: real man, real woman, and the bridal canopy, which stands for heaven and for Eden, is a prayer shawl stretched on four poles: groom and bride rejoice not as metaphor but as fact. Then (in the received tradition), immediately leaving the canopy, they head for bed, then for celebration. In the innocent world in which sexual relations commence after the marriage, a rite known as *yihud,* solitary converse of bride and groom all by themselves for the first time, is provided for, and to this the conclusion to the final blessing refers:

Praised are You, O Lord, who causes the groom to rejoice with his bride.

These Seven Blessings say nothing of private people and of their anonymous falling in love. Nor do they speak of the community of Israel, as one might expect on a public occasion. Lover and beloved rather are transformed from natural to mythical figures. The blessings speak of archetypical Israel, represented here and now by the bride and groom. All becomes credible not by what is said but by what is felt: that joy, that sense of witness to what we ourselves experience—these are the two ingredients that transform. The natural events of human life—here, the marriage of ordinary folk—are by myth heightened into a re-enactment of Israel's life as a people. In marriage, individuals stand in the place of mythic figures, yet remain, after all, a boy and a girl. What gives their love its true meaning is their acting out the myth of creation, revelation, and redemption, here and now embodied in that love. But in the end, the sacred and the secular are in most profane, physical love united.

The wedding of symbol and everyday reality—the fusion and confusion of the two—these mark the classical Judaic enchantment that turns into metaphor the natural and human sentiment, the joy of marriage. Invoking creation, Adam and Eve, the Garden of Eden, and the historical memory of the this-worldly destruction of an old, unexceptional temple, the private is turned public, the individual made paradigm. Ordinary events, such as a political and military defeat or success, are changed into theological categories, such as divine punishment and heavenly compassion. If religion is a means of ultimate transformation, rendering the commonplace into the paradigmatic, changing the here and now into a moment of eternity and of eternal return, then the marriage liturgy serves to exemplify what is *religious* in Judaic existence. Time, space, action as these touch the passage of life lived one by one, the meal, the birth, the marriage—all are transformed through community, by which, we now realize, Judaism means the communion of the ages, the shared being of all who have lived in Israel and as Israel.

PART II
Rites of the Group

CHAPTER 5

The Passover *Seder:*
"To See Ourselves As If…"

THE SINGLE most widely practiced rite of Judaism in North America requires family and friends to sit down for supper. How so secular an act is turned from a supper party into a highly charged occasion, rich in deeply felt meanings, we would not find out if we were simply to review the words that are said, any more than the formula of *Kol Nidre* ("All vows . . .") explains the wonder of the theater into which, on the eve of the Day of Atonement, the synagogue is turned. The choreography, the bits and pieces of drama, music, song, procession, display of self-evidently eloquent symbols—all of these by themselves do not account for the power and magic of either *Kol Nidre* or the Passover *seder.* The meal consumed with ceremony turns people into something other than what they think they are, and puts them down square in the path of an onrushing history. In the presence of symbols both visual and verbal, in the formation of family and friends into an Israel redeemed from Egypt, people become something else—a wonder worked by words.

At the festival of Passover (or *Pessah*), which coincides with the first full moon after the vernal equinox, Jewish families gather around their tables for a holy meal. There—speaking in very general terms—they retell the story of the Exodus from Egypt in times long past. With unleavened bread and sanctified wine, they celebrate the liberation of slaves from Pharaoh's bondage. At this rite, a single formula captures the moment—here we begin, if we are to understand how the *we* of the family becomes the *we* of Israel, how the eternal and perpetual coming of spring is made to mark a singular moment, a one-time act on the stage in the unfolding of linear time:

> For ever after, in every generation, *every Israelite must think of himself or herself as having gone forth from Egypt.* [Italics added]

A curious passage indeed! It is one thing to tell Jews to think of themselves in one way, rather than in some other. It is quite a different thing to explain why Jews respond to the demand—and they do respond.

As is my way, I start with the here and the now of everyday experience. What, for nearly all Jews all over the world, makes plausible the statement *"We* went forth . . ."? And why do people sit down for supper and announce, "It was not only our forefathers that the Holy One, blessed be He, redeemed. *Us, too, the living,* He redeemed together with them"? I cannot imagine a less plausible statement, a more compelling invitation to derision and disbelief. We were not there. Pharaoh has been dead for quite some time. Egypt languishes in the rubbish heap of history. Wherein the enchantment? Why us? Why here? Why now? The answer derives from the power, within Judaism, through enchantment to transform the here and now into an intimation of the wholly other. In seeing the everyday as metaphor, we perceive that deeper layer of meaning that permits us to treat as obvious and self-evident the transforming power of comparison, of simile applied to oneself: let's pretend, and what if? and why not?

When things are not the way they seem, it is because we have already concluded that beyond the here and now there must be a something else. That is how metaphor does its work. Enchantment calls up a spirit already present and within. Hunger and satisfaction stand for exile and redemption; the birth of a child brings Elijah into my home; and when Suzanne and I got married, we stood for Adam and Eve entering Eden and Zion restored in God's good time. In all these occasions for transformation, I found I was someone else, somewhere else, some time other than now. The *we* of family, too—as in our initial encounter with this rather odd occasion of a family meal eaten in the shadow of the pyramids—is told it is someone else, somewhere else, in another time and another place. And this enchantment can, I think, occur only because the family and friends now assembled have in mind and imagination already transformed themselves. Then they can be told to change and instructed in their roles. If we review the provocative themes of the script for the drama, we may pick out those components of the everyday that are subjected to transformation.

One theme stands out, which I may state in this way: we, here and now, are really living then and there. So, for example:

We were slaves of Pharaoh in Egypt and the Lord our God brought us forth from there with a mighty hand and an outstretched arm. And if the Holy One, blessed be He, had not brought our fathers forth from Egypt, then we and our descendants would still be slaves to Pharaoh in Egypt. And so, even if all of us were full of wisdom, understanding, sages and well informed in the Torah, we should still be obligated to repeat again the story of the Exodus from Egypt; and whoever treats as an important matter the story of the Exodus from Egypt is praiseworthy.

And again:

This is the bread of affliction which our ancestors ate in the land of Egypt. Let all who are hungry come and eat with us, let all who are needy come and celebrate the Passover with us. This year here, next year in the land of Israel; this year slave, next year free people.

And yet a third statement:

This is the promise which has stood by our forefathers and stands by us. For neither once, nor twice, nor three times was our destruction planned; in every generation they rise against us, and in every generation God delivers us from their hands into freedom, out of anguish into joy, out of mourning into festivity, out of darkness into light, out of bondage into redemption.

Enchantment is not subtle. As though the implicit premise were not clear, let us revert to the point at which we began and hear it stated in so many words:

For ever after, in every generation, *every Israelite must think of himself or herself as having gone forth from Egypt.* For we read in the Torah: "In that day thou shalt teach thy son, saying: All this is because of what God did for me when I went forth from Egypt." It was not only our forefathers that the Holy One, blessed be He, redeemed; us too, the living, He redeemed together with them, as we learn from the verse in the Torah: "And He brought us out from thence, so that He might bring us home, and give us the land which he pledged to our forefathers." [Italics added]

There is nothing subtle about rites of transformation. We are never left in doubt about *who* we are now supposed to be, or *where,* or *when,* or *why.*

If we ask, therefore, what experience in the here and the now is taken up and transformed by enchantment into the then and the there, we move from the rite to the reality. That progress tells us what troubles these people, and makes playacting plausible as they turn their lives into metaphor, themselves into actors, the everyday into pretense and drama. The question takes on urgency when we remind ourselves that we confront the single most popular and widely observed rite of Judaism. What speaks so ubiquitously, with such power, that pretty much everybody who wants to joins in? In my view, the message penetrates to the hearts of people who remember the murder, in the near past, of six million Jews, and who know that today they, too, are a minority and at risk, if not in politics then in psychology.

What troubles Jews in a free society is not that they are not free, but that they are uncomfortable with the kind of freedom that makes them what they are: free to be different. And who wants to be different? When, as we shall see, synagogue Judaism announces who is Israel, difference turns into destiny. But the rite of a family occasion is different: it appeals as synagogue Judaism does not, and makes a powerful statement to the individual and family in particular. I think the reason is that the rite transforms what people feel into a sentiment they can recognize; they become a metaphor for something more—and more noble—than what they feel. In theoretical language, Jews in North America drawn to their dinner parties enter an anguish drawn from mythic being because that anguish imparts to their ordinary life a metaphoric quality that makes sense of the already perceived.

The Jews are a minority, small in numbers, compensating in visibility. So far as they differ from "the others," a fantasized majority alike in all respects because everyone not Jewish is the same—that is, is (merely) gentile—Jews confront not a critical but a chronic discomfort. To be different—whatever the difference—requires explanation; it provokes resentment; it creates tension demanding resolution and pain requiring remission. For the young, difference is deadly. For the middle-aged, difference demands explanation and compensation, and may well exact the cost of diminished opportunity. For the individual may not be different from other individuals, but families always do retain that mark of difference from other families, and that in the very nature of their existence. Passover celebrates the family of Israel and is celebrated by the families of Israel. So Passover, with its rhetoric of rejoicing for freedom, plays out in a minor key the song of liberation: today slaves, next year, free; today here, next year in Jerusalem (that is, not the real Jerusalem but the imagined, heavenly one). That is why, when they read that they must see themselves "as having gone forth from Egypt"—that is, *as if*—they do not burst out laughing and call for the main course.

When people tell themselves that they, too, were slaves but have been freed, the words invoke the metaphor of the Israelites in Egypt to refer to the real world of Jews in the world today. These people, I think, find deeply troubling a principal side to their existence, so troubling that they invoke it, deny it, celebrate its end in ancient times—and fervently ask that it come to a conclusion once again. Obviously, it is not slavery. The freedom that Jews celebrate—but also seek (so the liturgy maintains)—is *from* as much as *to:* from one thing, to do some other. Let us go back over the language of the Passover narrative once again:

> We were slaves in Egypt . . . and if the Holy One had not . . . we would still be slaves. . . .
> This year here slaves here, next year free in Jerusalem.
> . . .
> In every generation they rise against us, and in every generation God delivers us. . . .
> For ever after, in every generation every Israelite must think of himself or herself as having gone forth from Egypt.
> . . .

Organized, socially acceptable paranoia? Alas, not at all. The facts of the history of the Jews over the centuries transform paranoia into understatement.

The key to the power of the Passover *seder* I find in the resentment expressed in the simple—and, alas, in my view self-evident—statement, "In every generation they rise against us." Somewhere, some time, that is always so. And if I had in one sentence to explain the extraordinary appeal of Passover, it is not in the mythic being invoked but in the this-worldly, factual statement: we are hated, we are in trouble, but God saves (or, something happens). Passover is popular now because it speaks to a generation that knows what the gentiles can do, having seen what they did to the Jews of Europe. Passover, furthermore, speaks not to history alone but to personal biography; it joins together history with the experience of the individual, because the individual as a minority finds self-evident—relevant, true, urgent—a rite that reaches into the everyday and the here and now and turns that common world into a metaphor for the reality of Israel, enslaved but also redeemed. Whether people see themselves as having gone forth from Egypt I cannot say. But I know that they see themselves as slaves in Egypt. And that is what draws them to the *seder:* it explains what, in the everyday, things mean beyond the four ells of the private person's world. In terms now familiar, the *seder* effects its enchantment by showing the individual that the everyday stands for something beyond; the here and now represents the everywhere and all the time: "In every generation they rise against us." True—but also God saves. Who would not be glad to have supper to celebrate that truth, if only through commemoration?

If the Passover *seder* banquet enchants the everyday experience of people under pressure, transforming what is personal and private into what is public and shared, nothing in the unfolding of the *seder* rite focuses upon that one message. As with *Kol Nidre,* in which the words speak of one thing, the music of something else, so here the words speak of many things, only sometimes coming to the main point. But the main point remains present throughout, because that one theme, the Exodus of Israel from Egypt, remains at the fore. The word *seder* means "order," and the sense is that a sequence of actions takes place as prescribed. Here is the order of the *seder.* The word *matzah* refers to unleavened bread. What we shall see is that same disjuncture between words and deeds, between declarations and inner sentiments, that I have noted of the *Kol Nidre* and the rite of the *huppah.* To make this clear I have divided the order into the gestures, on the one side; the recitation of words, indented and in italics, on the other:

The Passover *Seder:* "To See Ourselves As If . . ."

Deeds
>   *words*

first washing of the hands
eating of the parsley
breaking of the middle cake of *matzah*
>   *recital of the narrative (Haggaddah)*

second washing of the hands
>   *grace for bread*

breaking and dividing up of topmost piece of *matzah*
eating of bitter herb dipped in *charoset* (chopped nuts, wine)
eating of bitter herb with *matzah*
meal
eating of the *afikomon* (a piece of *matzah* eaten to mark the end of the meal)
>   *Grace after Meals*
>   *Hallel (recitation of Psalms 113–18)*
>   *closing prayer*

The curious picture emerges of two quite separate occasions, running side by side but not meeting. Were we to describe the banquet on the basis of this catalogue, we should expect a recitation much engaged by attention to hand washing, the eating of parsley, the breaking and disposition of pieces of unleavened bread—in all, raising and lowering, breaking and hiding and eating, pieces of *matzah*. We should then be unprepared for the reality of the *seder* rite, which involves an enormous flow of words. Not only so, but the introit of the rite focuses upon the ritual aspect of the meal, not on the narrative:

Why has this night been made different from all other nights? On all other nights we eat bread whether leavened

[77]

or unleavened, on this night only unleavened; on all other nights we eat all kinds of herbs, on this night only bitter ones; on all other nights we do not dip herbs even once; on this night, twice; on all other nights we sit at the table either sitting or reclining, on this night we all recline.

In point of fact, none of these questions, addressed by the youngest present to the presiding officer, is ever answered. Instead we get the following (I italicize the operative words):

We were slaves of Pharaoh in Egypt; and the Lord our God brought us forth from there with a mighty hand and an outstretched arm. And if the Holy One, blessed be He, had not brought our fathers forth from Egypt, then surely we, and our children, and our children's children, would be enslaved to Pharaoh in Egypt. *And so, even if all of us were full of wisdom and understanding, well along in years and deeply versed in the tradition, we should still be bidden to repeat once more the story of the exodus from Egypt; and he who delights to dwell on the liberation is one to be praised.*

Now we shift from the symbols present to the occasion commemorated and celebrated; and a considerable "narrative" makes us forget the pillow and the parsley and the *matzah* and remember Pharaoh and Egypt. This narrative is composed of bits and pieces which all together do not flow together at all, a citation and exegesis of some verses of Scripture, some games, prayers, snatches of stories, hymns. Made up of incoherent liturgies, joining together varieties of essentially unrelated material, the so-called narrative does tell this story, and I take it to form the centerpiece of the whole:

[78]

The Passover *Seder:* "To See Ourselves As If . . ."

Long ago our ancestors were idol-worshippers but now the Holy One has drawn us to his service. So we read in the Torah: And Joshua said to all the people, "Thus says the Lord, God of Israel: From time immemorial your fathers lived beyond the river Euphrates, even to Terah, father of Abraham and of Nahor, and they worshipped idols. And I took your father Abraham from beyond the river and guided his footsteps throughout the land of Canaan. I multiplied his offspring and gave him Isaac. To Isaac I gave Jacob and Esau. And I set apart Mount Seir as the inheritance of Esau, while Jacob and his sons went down to Egypt."

I remind you where we are: sitting around a table; family and friends at a banquet. More surprising than Elijah's visit at the birth rite of circumcision is the advent of our idol-worshiping ancestors. None of this pertains to the occasion. All of it is deeply relevant to those present, for it says who they (really) are, and for whom they really stand. They in the here and now stand for "our ancestors"—Abraham, Isaac, and Jacob. That is the first part.

Here is the second, and more important (the key words italicized):

Blessed is *he who keeps his promise to Israel, for the Holy One, set a term to our bondage,* fulfilling the word which he gave our father Abraham in the covenant made between the divided sacrifice: Know beyond a doubt that your offspring will be *strangers in a land that is not theirs,* four hundred years they shall serve and suffer. But in the end I shall pronounce judgment on the oppressor people and your offspring shall go forth with great wealth.

[79]

We are dealing with people who respond to the description of their circumstance here: strangers in a land that is not theirs, indeed! That is bad sociology—and, for the free Jews of the Western democracies, worse politics. But in here, in the heart, it not only rings true; it is true: *strangers in a land that is not theirs,* not because the neighbors are enemies, but because the Jews are different from the neighbors, and that suffices. Canada and America are as much theirs as anyone else's, but still: *strangers in a land that is not theirs.* They could, of course, migrate to a land that *is* theirs (within its civil myth)— namely, the State of Israel. But they do not—and yet they say, "This year here slaves here, next year free in Jerusalem." There is a jarring unreality to the entire drama. Through the natural eye, one sees ordinary folk, not much different from their neighbors in dress, language, or aspirations. The words they speak do not describe reality, and are not meant to. When Jews say of themselves, "We were the slaves of Pharaoh in Egypt," they know they never felt the lash; but through the eye of faith, that is just what they have done. It is *their* liberation, not merely that of long-dead forebears, they now celebrate.

Here lies the power of the Passover banquet rite to transform ordinary existence into an account of something beyond. Ordinary existence imposes its tensions. Jews are different from gentiles, and thus are defined as Jews. But now, in the transformation at hand, to be a Jew means to be a slave who has been liberated by God. To be Israel means to give eternal thanks for God's deliverance. And that deliverance is not at a single moment in historical time. Transformed into a permanent feature of reality, it is made myth: that story of deep truth that comes true in every generation and is always celebrated. Here again, events of natural, ordinary life are transformed through myth into paradigmatic, eternal, and ever-recurrent sacred moments. In terms I have used before, the everyday is treated as paradigm and metaphor. Jews think of themselves as having gone forth from Egypt, and Scripture so instructs them. God did not redeem the dead generation of the Exodus alone, but the living, too—especially the living. Thus, the family states:

> Again and again, in double and redoubled measure, are we beholden to God the All-Present: that He freed us from the Egyptians and wrought His judgment on them; that He sentenced all their idols and slaughtered all their first-born; that He gave their treasure to us and split the Red Sea for us; that He led us through it dry-shod and drowned the tyrants in it; that He helped us through the desert and fed us with the manna; that He gave the Sabbath to us and brought us to Mount Sinai; that He gave the Torah to us and brought us to our homeland—there to build the Temple for us, for atonement of our sins.

Israel was born in historical times. Historians, biblical scholars, and archeologists have much to say about that event. But to the classical Jew, their findings, while interesting, have little bearing on the meaning of reality. The redemptive promise that stood by the forefathers and "stands by us" is not a mundane historical event but a mythic interpretation of historical, natural events. Oppression, homelessness, extermination—like salvation, homecoming, renaissance—are this-worldly and profane, supplying headlines for newspapers. The myth that a Jew must think of himself or herself as having gone forth from Egypt, and as being redeemed by God, renders ordinary experience into a moment of celebration. If "us, too, the living, He [has] redeemed," then the observer witnesses no longer only historical men in historical time, but an eternal return to sacred time.

Having come this far, we cannot evade the issue implicit in celebration of the Exodus: How long, and when, and by whom? That is to say, the enchantment transforms not only the here and now of the meal, but also the view of time ahead, the age beyond the next horizon. For what, after all, does the *seder* have to say about Israel's ongoing history? Is it merely a succession of meaningless disasters—worldly happenings without end or purpose? The answer comes in a folksong sung at the Passover *seder,* the ceremonial meal commemorating the Exodus from Egypt:

> An only kid, an only kid
> My father bought for two pennies,
> An only kid, an only kid.
> But along came the cat and ate up the kid,
> My father bought for two pennies,
> An only kid, an only kid.

And so goes the dreary story. Here is the final verse:

> Then the Holy One, blessed be He, came along
> And slew the angel of death
> Who slew the slaughterer
> Who slew the ox
> Who drank the water
> That put out the fire
> That burned the stick
> That beat the dog
> That bit the cat
> That ate the kid

The Passover *Seder:* "To See Ourselves As If . . ."

My father had bought for two pennies,
An only kid, an only kid.

One damn thing after another? Yes—but, then, no. The his-
toɪy of Israel, the Jewish people, is the history of the only kid;
at the end, the Holy One, blessed be He, comes to slaughter
the angel of death, to vindicate the long sufferings of many
centuries, and to bring to a happy and joyful end the times of
trouble.

Here is the whole of Israel's history embodied in the little
lamb the father bought for next to nothing—his only kid. The
fate of Israel, the lamb slaughtered not once but many times
over, is suffering that has an end and a purpose in the end of
days. Death will die, and all who shared in the lamb's suffering
will witness the divine dénouement of history. The history of
sin, suffering, atonement, reconciliation is a cycle not destined
forever and ever to repeat itself. To hear such a message—
deriving from and yet transcending one's everyday experience—will people not gladly come for supper? What unites
the discrete, unrelated events in the life of the "only kid" and
provokes a singular response among varied men is the perva-
sive conviction that an end is coming. Nothing is meaningless,
for the random happenings of the centuries are in truth leading
to the Messiah. The messianic hope lies at the end of the mythic
life of Israel and illuminates every moment in it. In the workaday terms important to us, people may not perceive meaning
in what happens to them, but they want to perceive it. That
is why the magic works. It is made to work by the power of
will and the force of imagination. These turn time from now
to history then and always, space from here to there, action
from resentment or fear of the outsider to slavery, then freedom, and—this above all—community made up out of family

and friends, all transformed into Israel. At the end, we remind ourselves, the Passover *seder* finds nearly all Jews in America and Canada, whether they call themselves religious or secular, around the banquet table. Its curious message speaks to us all. But then, on the morrow, when the synagogue opens its door, most, though not all, Jews find themselves somewhere else. That puzzling act of selectivity will, in due course, receive its explanation.

CHAPTER 6

Sabbaths of Creation, Festivals of Redemption: Turning from the World to Rest

THE Passover *seder* is nearly universally observed. Not so the Sabbath, that day of rest, marked by prayer and study of the Torah, by relaxation and enjoyment from sunset to sunset. Not so the Sabbath, which yet forms the centerpiece of the Judaic way of life. For the words heard and spoken on the Sabbath, while transforming time from one order to some other, while changing what it means to live, are not alone enough. This is a paradox that holds as well for public synagogal aspects of the festivals, of the holy Days of Awe.

The great theologian Abraham Joshua Heschel has spelled out the human transformation accomplished by the Sabbath:

> Judaism is a religion of time aiming at the sanctification of time. Unlike the space-minded man to whom time is unvaried, iterative, homogeneous, to whom all hours are alike . . . , the Bible senses the diversified character of time.

There are no two hours alike. Every hour is unique and the only one given at the moment, exclusive and endlessly precious. Judaism teaches us to be attached to holiness in time, to be attached to sacred events, to learn how to consecrate sanctuaries that emerge from the magnificent stream of a year. The Sabbaths are our great cathedrals, and our Holy of Holies is a shrine that neither the Romans nor the Germans were able to burn. . . . Jewish ritual may be characterized as the art of significant forms in time, as architecture of time. Most of its observances . . . depend on a certain hour of the day or season of the year. . . . The main themes of faith lie in the realm of time. We remember the day of the exodus from Egypt, the day when Israel stood at Sinai; and our Messianic hope is the expectation of a day, of the end of days.[1]

Contrast the Sabbath and the occasion of Passover. Passover is once a year, not every week. Passover stands in judgment against others—the outsider—and gives resonance to legitimate resentment. Passover is like a love affair—intense but brief. The Sabbath stands in judgment upon us as human beings and calls into question the things that should merely engage but, in fact, overwhelm us. That is why, at sunset on the eve of the seventh day, words do not create worlds, except for a tiny sector of Israel, that special entity of Orthodoxy. The magic works only when people want it to. The Sabbath is like a marriage that is ordinary and lasts for years. A love affair is what it is—but on the basis of the Sabbath, one can build one's life, and many do.

We Jews fail the Sabbath, fail to observe the day of rest and renewal, not because in the ordinary and everyday we do not find an above and beyond. The opposite is the case. The common life of every day demands the Sabbath; the workaday world requires it; the working person languishes without it. But the Sabbath's magic and message of the sanctification of time—remarkably relevant, as we shall see, to the human condition at the threshold of the twenty-first century—present a vision altogether too austere, too penetrating. Lacking in sentimental guise, the Sabbath does not appeal to resentment and fear—transient emotions that require legitimation and exorcism, too—and does not address individual and family alone.

The Sabbath lays down a judgment on the fundamental issues of our civilization and, specifically, demands restraint, dignity, reticence, and silent rest—not commonplace virtues. If, therefore, the transformation of time, the centerpiece of the life of Judaism, occurs for only a few, the reason is not obsolescence but the opposite: excessive relevance. The Sabbath touches too close to home, ripping the raw nerve of reality. For it calls into question the foundations of the life of one dimension only, asking how people can imagine that all there is is what they see just now. The Judaic vision that perceives things to be not what they seem blinds, on the Sabbath, with too much light. Circumcision is once in a while; the meal is eaten, mostly, without benefit of blessing, except on cultic occasions; the *huppah* for the fortunate is once or, at most, twice, and how hard is it to pretend we are Adam and Eve anyhow; and the Passover is but once a year and, in all the hocus-pocus of removing leaven and eating *matzah,* easy in its cultic complexity. But the Sabbath, and, in its wake, the festivals and the Days of Awe—these are another matter. They question. They disrupt. They do condemn. And they take place every week—or, with the festivals, more often—turning one place into another and one time into another.

To mark the transformation of time through the enchantment of sanctification into holy time, special time, synagogues announce "services," but not many people come. And anyhow, services alone are not the Sabbath, unless people keep the twenty-four hours from Friday's sunset through Saturday's. True, rabbis plead with people to honor the Sabbath day. But few listen. The rabbi, in preaching about the Sabbath, goes through a ritual of making people feel bad about themselves, but good about their rabbi.

The Sabbath words yield no new worlds, not because people do not listen to the answer that the Sabbath gives in the way they listen to the answer of Passover. It is that they do not ask the question that the Sabbath answers, while they do find urgent the question settled by Passover. The Sabbath in its depths addresses a profound human problem: one of public policy, nothing less. The Sabbath confronts civilization and concerns the world at large, not the Jews alone. When people wish to take up this problem, they will enter the sacred disciplines of the Sabbath as commonly as they join the Passover banquet.

The problem of the Sabbath concerns that fundamental trait of mind with which I commenced: the capacity to see things as other than they appear to be. The Sabbath—therefore also the festivals—does not celebrate but rather exercises that human gift. But what we are supposed to see beyond what we do see requires definition—and thus we return to the great exposition of Abraham Joshua Heschel on the meaning of the Sabbath for humanity. He shows us how to move from the words to the worlds they create, to turn the notes into music— or, at least, to know that the notes stand for music. Heschel's theology of the Sabbath contrasts the perceived world of space with the imagined world of time:

Sabbaths of Creation, Festivals of Redemption

The solution to mankind's most vexing problem will not be found in renouncing technical civilization, but in attaining some degree of independence of it. In regard to external gifts, to outward possessions, there is only one proper attitude—to have them and to be able to do without them. On the Sabbath we live . . . independent of technical civilization: we abstain primarily from any activity that aims at remaking or reshaping the things of space. Man's royal privilege to conquer nature is suspended on the seventh day.[2]

Heschel comes right to the heart of matters. Modern civilization requires the Sabbath far more urgently than did those Jews who kept the day from Sinai forward, because the Sabbath, with its rest and renunciation, draws us back from engagement with things, with space. It suspends for a day our conquest of nature and precipitates for that same day the praise and celebration of nature. For the Sabbath celebrates the completion and perfection of creation, that is, of nature:

When the heaven and earth were done, and all their array, when God had finished the work that he had been doing, then he rested on the seventh day from all the work that he had done. Then God blessed the seventh day and made it holy, because on it God desisted from all of the work of creating in which he had been engaged. (Genesis 2:1–3)

This account of the first Sabbath stands in judgment on those who, like God, create but, unlike God, never rest, who deny themselves occasion to admire and enjoy. I can find no more penetrating judgment upon the human condition than the

[89]

Sabbath's: one can have too much, enjoy too little, and so care about things that do not count:

> Inner liberty depends upon being exempt from domination of things as well as from domination of people. There are many who have acquired a high degree of political and social liberty, but only very few are not enslaved to things. This is our constant problem—how to live with people and remain free, how to live with things and remain independent.[3]

The words that at sunset on Friday transform the world and bring into being a different world do their work only when we want them to. But no message can find a less endearing welcome than one that questions the one-sidedness of the life of things and material achievement. The Sabbath speaks of transcendent things, of life with God and in God, in ways in which the more concrete celebration of freedom does not. For the Sabbath penetrates into the heart of commonplace being, while Passover addresses the merely social and political. Societies do well with the latter kind of problem, working to change matters to suit them through the power of the will. In a world that celebrates deed, not deliberation, that reckons value in what is weighed and measured, how can words create the intangible world of time?

> We cannot solve the problem of time through the conquest of space, through either pyramids or fame. We can only solve the problem of time through sanctification of time. To men alone time is elusive; to men with God time is eternity in disguise. This is the task of men: to conquer space and sanctify time. We must conquer space in order to

sanctify time. All week long we are called upon to sanctify life through employing things of space. On the Sabbath it is given us to share in the holiness that is in the heart of time.[4]

From the issue of intellect we turn to the everyday: Why not ask the question that the Sabbath answers? Heschel's account of that question—Are things merely what they seem to be?—cuts to the core of that Judaic perspective that denies that the everyday is all there is:

> In our daily lives we attend primarily to that which the senses are spelling out for us: to what the eyes perceive, to what the fingers touch. Reality to us is thinghood, consisting of substances that occupy space; even God is considered by most of us a thing. The result of our thinginess is our blindness to all reality that fails to identify itself as a thing, as a matter of fact. This is obvious in our understanding of time, which, being thingless and insubstantial, appears to us as if it had no reality.[5]

The words that precipitate the world of the Sabbath invoke the day both as a memorial of creation and as a remembrance of the redemption from Egypt. The primary liturgy of the Sabbath is the reading of the Scripture lesson from the Torah in the synagogue service. So the three chief themes of the Judaic system—creation, revelation, and redemption—are combined in the weekly observance of the seventh day. The Sabbath works more than through words: it is the creation also of one's actions and omissions in making of time a different world. The Sabbath is protected by negative rules: one must not work; one must not pursue mundane concerns. But the

Sabbath is also adorned with less concrete but affirmative laws: one must rejoice; one must rest.

How to make and keep the Sabbath? All week long I look forward to it, and the anticipation enhances the ordinary days. Usually, by Friday afternoon, those who keep the Sabbath will have bathed, put on their Sabbath garments, and set aside the affairs of the week. At home, the family—husband, wife, children, or whoever stands for family—will have cleaned, cooked, and arranged the finest table. It is common to invite guests for the Sabbath meals. The Sabbath comes at sunset and leaves when three stars appear Saturday night. After a brief service, the family comes together to enjoy its best meal of the week—a meal at which particular Sabbath foods are served. In the morning comes the Sabbath service—including a public reading from the Torah, the Five Books of Moses, and prophetic writings—and an additional service in memory of the Temple sacrifices on Sabbaths of old. Then home for lunch and commonly a Sabbath nap, the sweetest part of the day. As the day wanes, the synagogue calls for a late afternoon service, followed by Torah study and a third meal. Then comes a ceremony, *havdalah* ("separation")—effected with spices, wine, and candlelight—between the holy time of the Sabbath and the ordinary time of weekday. I do not mean to suggest that this idyllic picture characterizes all Sabbath observance, nor do I believe (though many Jews do) that the only way to sanctify the Sabbath is in the received way I have described. Reform Judaism has displayed the wisdom to honor, as an act of sanctification of the time of the Sabbath, a variety of abstinences and actions. But, in the main, the Sabbath works its wonder when people retreat into family—however they understand family—and take leave of work and the workaday world.

Sabbaths of Creation, Festivals of Redemption

This simple, regular observance has elicited endless praise. To the Sabbath-observing Jew, the Sabbath is the chief sign of God's grace:

> For thou hast chosen us and sanctified us above all nations, in love and favor has given us thy holy Sabbath as an inheritance.

So is sanctified the Sabbath wine. Likewise in the Sabbath-morning liturgy:

> You did not give it [Sabbath] to the nations of the earth, nor did you make it the heritage of idolators, nor in its rest will unrighteous men find a place.
> But to Israel your people you have given it in love, to the seed of Jacob whom you have chosen, to that people who sanctify the Sabbath day. All of them find fulfillment and joy from your bounty.
> For the seventh day did you choose and sanctify as the most pleasant of days and you called it a memorial to the works of creation.

Here again we find a profusion of themes, this time centered upon the Sabbath. The Sabbath is a sign of the covenant. It is a gift of grace, which neither idolators nor evil people may enjoy. It is the testimony of the chosenness of Israel. And it is the most pleasant of days. Keeping the Sabbath *is* living in God's kingdom:

> Those who keep the Sabbath and call it a delight will rejoice in your kingdom.

So states the additional Sabbath prayer. Keeping the Sabbath now is a foretaste of the redemption: "This day is for Israel light and rejoicing." The rest of the Sabbath is, as the afternoon prayer affirms:

> a rest granted in generous love, a true and faithful rest. . . .
> Let your children realize that their rest is from you, and by their rest may they sanctify your name.

That people need respite from the routine of work is no discovery of the Judaic tradition. But that the way in which Jews accomplish this routine change of pace may be made the very heart and soul of spiritual existence is the single absolutely unique element in Judaic tradition. The word *Sabbath* simply renders the Hebrew *Shabbat;* it does not translate it, for there is no translation. In no other tradition or culture can an equivalent word be found. Certainly those who compare the Sabbath of Judaism to the somber, supposedly joyless Sunday of the Calvinists know nothing of what the Sabbath has meant and continues to mean to Jews.

What, precisely, does the Sabbath expect of us? And how, if we say the words and mean them, do we find the Sabbath as the answer and the way of life of the ordinary person? Heschel answers these questions when he describes the Sabbath as a work of art:

> Labor is a craft, but perfect rest is an art. It is the result of an accord of body, mind and imagination. . . . The seventh day is a palace in time, which we build. It is made of soul, of joy and reticence. In its atmosphere a discipline is a reminder of adjacency to eternity. Indeed, the splendor

of the day is expressed in terms of abstentions, just as the mystery of God is more adequately conveyed . . . in the categories of negative theology which claims that we can never say what he is, we can only say when he is not.

Heschel finds in the Sabbath "the day on which we are called upon to share in what is eternal in time, to turn from the world of creation to the creations of the world."[6]

From this brief description of what the Jew actually does on the seventh day, we can hardly come to understand how the Sabbath can have meant so much as to elicit such words as those of the Jewish prayerbook and of Rabbi Heschel. Those words, like the negative laws of the Sabbath—not to mourn, not to confess sins, not to repent, not to do anything that might lead to unhappiness—describe something only the participant can truly comprehend and feel. Only a family whose life focuses upon the Sabbath week by week, year by year, from birth to death, can know the sanctity of which the theologian speaks, the sacred rest to which the prayers refer. The heart and soul of the Judaic tradition, the Sabbath, cannot be described: it can only be experienced. For the student of religions, it stands as that element of Judaism that is absolutely unique and, therefore, a mystery. It forms the heart of the enchanted life of Judaism: *where* and *how* and *why* Judaism is a religion, not merely a social entity or a politics or a culture or a way of life. For transformation speaks not of external things but of a change at the very core of being: there is religion; there, in the language of Judaism, is the Torah; there we meet God; there we become like God: "in our image, after our likeness."

The festivals, too, mark the passage of time: not of the week but of the seasons. These seasons of sanctification and celebration are three: *Sukkot,* the week following the first full moon after the autumnal equinox, alluded to in classical sources as the "Festival," the one above all others; *Pessah,* or Passover, the week following the first full moon after the vernal equinox (see chapter 5); and *Shavuot,* or the Feast of Weeks, seven weeks later. Each festival both celebrates and commemorates: celebrating an event in nature, commemorating an event in Israel's sacred history.

Sukkot, the Feast of Tabernacles, marks the end of agricultural toil. The fall crops by then are gathered in from field, orchard, and vineyard. The rainy season in the Holy Land of Israel—and, in North America, the winter—is about to begin. It is time both to give thanks for what has been granted and to pray for abundant rains in the coming months. Called "festival of the ingathering," *Sukkot* is the celebration of nature. But the mode of celebration, also after the fact, commemorates a moment in Israel's history—specifically, the wandering in the wilderness. Then the Israelites lived not in permanent houses but in huts or shedlike stalls, or booths. At a time of bounty, it is good to be reminded of the travail of men and women and their dependence upon heavenly succor, which underlines the message of the Sabbath. The principal observance of the Festival is still the construction of a frail hut, or booth, for temporary use during the festival. In it in warmer climates, Jews eat their meals out of doors. The huts are covered over with branches, leaves, fruit, and flowers, but light shows through, and, at night, the stars.

This brings us back to Passover. But now we see the festival in its own setting, rather than in ours. We know the words, and I have explained why people so say them as to make a world. But what world do they call into being? Passover is the Jewish spring festival, and the symbols of the Passover *seder*— hard-boiled eggs and vegetable greens, lying on a plate on the

seder table but curiously neglected in the Passover narrative—
are not unfamiliar in other spring rites. Here, however, the
spring rite has been transformed into a historical commemoration. The natural course of the year, while important, is subor-
dinated to the historical events remembered and relived on the
festival. Called the "feast of unleavened bread" and the season
of our freedom, the Passover festival preserves ancient rites in
a new framework.

It is, for example, absolutely prohibited to make use of
leaven, fermented dough, and the like. The agricultural calendar of ancient Canaan was marked by the grain harvest, beginning in the spring with the cutting of barley and ending with
the reaping of the wheat approximately seven weeks later. The
farmers would get rid of all their sour dough, which they used
as yeast, and old bread as well as any leaven from last year's
crop. The origins of the practice are not clear, but that the
Passover taboo against leaven was connected with the agricultural calendar is beyond doubt. Just as the agricultural festivals
were historicized, likewise much of the detailed observance
connected with them was supplied with historical "reasons" or
explanations. In the case of the taboo against leaven, widely
observed today even among otherwise unobservant Jews, the
reason was that the Israelites, having to leave Egypt in haste,
had therefore to take with them unleavened bread, for they
had not time to permit the bread to rise properly and be baked.
Therefore we eat the *matzah,* unleavened bread.

The Feast of Weeks, *Shavuot* or Pentecost, comes seven
weeks after Passover. In the ancient Palestinian agricultural
calendar, *Shavuot* marked the end of the grain harvest and was
called the "feast of harvest." In Temple times, two loaves of
bread were baked from the wheat of the new crop and offered
as a sacrifice—the firstfruits of the wheat harvest. So *Shavuot*

came to be called the "day of the firstfruits." Judaism added a historical explanation to the natural ones derived from the land and its life: the rabbis held that the Torah was revealed on Mount Sinai on that day, and celebrated it as "the time of the giving of our Torah." Nowadays, in Reform and Conservative synagogues, the confirmation or graduation ceremonies of religious schools take place on *Shavuot.*

The three historical-agricultural festivals pertain, in varying ways and combinations, to the themes I have already considered. Passover is the festival of redemption and points toward the Torah revelation of the Feast of Weeks; the harvest festival in the autumn celebrates not only creation but especially redemption. Like the Sabbath, these festivals take ordinary people and turn them into Israel: they profane time and sanctify it. The same reason that accounts for the neglect of the Sabbath explains the limited popularity of the Festival, *Sukkot;* the Feast of Weeks, *Shavuot;* and the observance of Passover other than its banquet, on the one side, and (far less commonly) the bread taboo, on the other. But at stake in holy time is holiness, the transformation of a world by reason of an occasion; and if God counts and weighs and takes account of numbers, then what does God make of Israel anyhow? In the comparison of size as of space, no magic works. But to change life—that is true enchantment. And the Sabbath and its counterpart festivals transform life through the reordering of time and space, the reconciliation of action and community at rest.

For if the Grace after Meals reaches into commonplace experience of hunger and satisfaction, if the rites of circumcision and of the *huppah* serve to transform joy from personal to public existence, then what shall we say of the Sabbath? Among the words that make things different, those of the Sabbath speak to the heart of matters: the human condition of having too much and keeping too little. That dilemma is to be resolved through the enchantment of sanctification. In the transformation of working day to Sabbath, humanity completes creation and, like God, rests on the seventh day, so sanctifying it. The human condition that asks, What are we, what is our worth? finds its answer on the Sabbath: we are like God, and we are worth the world.

CHAPTER 7

The Days of Awe:
Israel before God

WHEN, in the late fall, the leaves turn color and the World
Series comes along, the world series of today's Judaism takes
place, too. Called in America the "High Holy Days," the Days
of Awe—ten momentous days from *Rosh Hashanah,* the New
Year, through *Yom Kippur,* the Day of Atonement—fill the
synagogues, like the pennant winners' ball parks, to overflow-
ing. Bare empty space on Sabbaths and festivals, the synagogues on the Days of Awe set the stage for mob scenes. And
that fact presents a puzzle. Clearly, Judaism does work its
enchantment and transforms some moments—some, but not
others. Since there are plenty of empty seats on the Sabbath
between the New Year and the Day of Atonement, as on all
other Sabbaths, it is not the season alone, any more than teams
without a shot at the pennant can fill a stadium in August. The
point is that the same Judaism, invoking the same symbolic
system and mythic structure, in some instances transforms but
in others changes nothing. If people respond to one rite and
not another, we ask what makes one rite compelling, another
irrelevant.

   As is our way, we listen first to the answer, then recover

the question, of the rite. Only then, having taken up the contents, may we seek an explanation in the larger context of contemporary Judaism and so explain why one set of words makes for enchantment, but with another set, nothing happens. When we can explain why this, not that, we shall have reached the end of our inquiry into the transformation that the received Judaism can, and cannot, accomplish. So to ask the question: What basic theory, framed in the heart and soul of the religious life of Judaism, explains the popularity of the Passover *seder,* which nearly everyone observes, and the neglect of the Sabbath, which nearly no one observes, and what moves people on Rosh Hashanah but not on the festival of *Sukkot,* following soon afterward?

First, let us listen with some care to the answers of the Days of Awe, for they will allow us to state the questions, from which, in our further step outward, we shall reach that larger social context that frames the whole. The New Year, Rosh Hashanah, and the Day of Atonement, Yom Kippur, together mark days of solemn penitence, at the start of the autumn festival season. These, in the prayers said on the occasion, are solemn times. The words of the liturgy specifically create a world of personal introspection, individual judgment. The turning of the year marks a time of looking backward. It is melancholy, like the falling leaves, but hopeful—even as with the pennant and the Series' losers: next year is another season.

The answer of the Days of Awe concerns life and death, which take mythic form in affirmations of God's rule and judgment. The words create a world aborning, the old now gone, the new just now arriving. The New Year, Rosh Hashanah, celebrates the creation of the world: *Today the world is born.* The time of new beginnings also marks endings: *On the New Year the decree is issued: Who will live and who will die?*

At the New Year—so the words state—humanity is inscribed for life or death in the heavenly books for the coming year; and on the Day of Atonement, the books are sealed. The world comes out to hear these words. The season is rich in celebration. The synagogues on that day are filled—whether with penitents or people who merely wish to be there hardly matters. The New Year is a day of remembrance on which the deeds of all creatures are reviewed. The principal themes of the words invoke creation, and God's rule over creation; revelation, and God's rule in the Torah for the created world; and redemption, God's ultimate plan for the world.

On the birthday of the world God made, God asserts His sovereignty, as in the New Year Prayer:

> Our God and God of our Fathers, Rule over the whole world in Your honor . . . and appear in Your glorious might to all those who dwell in the civilization of Your world, so that everything made will know that You made it, and every creature discern that You have created him, so that all in whose nostrils is breath may say, "The Lord, the God of Israel is king, and His kingdom extends over all."

Liturgical words concerning divine sovereignty, divine memory, and divine disclosure correspond to creation, revelation, and redemption. Sovereignty is established by creation of the world. Judgment depends upon law: "From the beginning You made this, Your purpose known." And therefore, since people have been told what God requires of them, they are judged:

> On this day sentence is passed upon countries, which to the sword and which to peace, which to famine and which

to plenty, and each creature is judged today for life or death. Who is not judged on this day? For the remembrance of every creature comes before You, each man's deeds and destiny, words and way.

These are strong words for people to hear. As life unfolds and people grow reflective, the Days of Awe seize the imagination: I live, I die, sooner or later it comes to all. The call for inner contemplation implicit in the mythic words elicits deep response.

The theme of revelation is further combined with redemption; the ram's horn, or *shofar,* which is sounded in the synagogue during daily worship for a month before the Rosh Hashanah festival, serves as a thread of unity connecting daily worship and the New Year:

> You did reveal yourself in a cloud of glory. . . . Out of heaven you made them [Israel] hear Your voice. . . . amid thunder and lightning You revealed yourself to them, and while the *shofar* sounded You shined forth upon them. . . . Our God and God of our fathers, sound the great *shofar* for our freedom. Lift up the ensign to gather our exiles. . . . Lead us happily to Zion Your city, Jerusalem the place of Your sanctuary.

The complex themes of the New Year, the most "theological" of Jewish holy occasions, thus weave together the tapestry of a highly charged moment in a world subject to the personal scrutiny of a most active God.

What of the Day of Atonement? Here, too, we hear the same answers, see the unfolding of a single process of transformation of secular into sacred time. Of the Days of Awe, the most personal, solemn, and moving is the Day of Atonement, Yom Kippur, the Sabbath of Sabbaths. It is marked by fasting and continuous prayer. On it, the Jew makes confession:

Our God and God of our fathers, may our prayer come before You. Do not hide yourself from our supplication, for we are not so arrogant or stiff-necked as to say before You, "We are righteous and have not sinned." But we have sinned.

We are guilt laden, we have been faithless, we have robbed. . . .

We have committed iniquity, caused unrighteousness, have been presumptuous. . . .

We have counseled evil, scoffed, revolted, blasphemed.

The Hebrew confession is built upon an alphabetical acrostic, as if God, who knows human secrets, will, by making certain every letter is represented, combine them into appropriate words. The very alphabet bears witness against us before God. Then:

What shall we say before You who dwell on high? What shall we tell You who live in heaven? Do You not know all things, both the hidden and the revealed? You know the secrets of eternity, the most hidden mysteries of life. You search the innermost recesses, testing men's feelings and heart. Nothing is concealed from You or hidden from Your eyes. May it therefore be Your will to forgive us our sins, to pardon us for our iniquities, to grant remission for our transgressions.

The Days of Awe: Israel before God

A further list of sins follows, composed on alphabetical lines. Prayers to be spoken by the congregation are all in the plural: "For the sin which we have sinned against You with the utterance of the lips. . . . for the sin which we have sinned before You openly and secretly." The community takes upon itself responsibility for what is done in it. All Israel is part of one community, one body; and all are responsible for the acts of each. The sins confessed are mostly against society, against one's fellowmen; few pertain to ritual laws. At the end comes a final word:

> O my God, before I was formed, I was nothing. Now that I have been formed, it is as though I had not been formed, for I am dust in my life, more so after death. Behold I am before You like a vessel filled with shame and confusion. May it be Your will . . . that I may no more sin, and forgive the sins I have already committed in Your abundant compassion.

While much of the liturgy speaks of "we," it focuses primarily on the individual, from beginning to end. The Days of Awe speak to the heart of the individual, telling a story of judgment and atonement. So the individual Jew stands before God: possessing no merits, yet hopeful of God's love and compassion. If that is the answer, can there be any doubt about the question? I think not. The power of the Days of Awe derives from the sentiments and emotions aroused by the theme of those days: What is happening to me? Where am I going?

Moments of introspection and reflection serve as guideposts in people's lives. That is why people treasure such moments and respond to the opportunities that define them. The themes of the Days of Awe stated in mythic terms address the human condition, and the message penetrates to the core of human concerns about life and death, the year past, the year beyond, the wrongs and the sins and the remissions and atonement. Now, viewed in context, the Days of Awe replay the music we hear on Sabbath and on festivals, on Passover and under the *huppah,* at the circumcision and at the Grace after Meals. No occasion within the liturgical life omits sanctification; none forgets salvation; none fails to speak of sanctification and salvation in the language of Torah and God's rule, creation, revelation, and redemption: Zion and Jerusalem; Abraham, Isaac, and Jacob; and on and on and on. A review of the range of public and communal celebration shows how profoundly integrated are the individual and the community, the private and the public blending into a single pattern of this-worldly sanctification aimed at salvation at the end of time.

In fact, like a fugue, the Judaic way of life joins into one harmony three distinct voices, three separate cycles; one voice in the rhythm of the year; the second voice in the rhythm of the week; the third voice in the rhythm of a person's life. A bird's-eye view of the whole will provide a vision that, in a moment, will allow the reader to discern why this, not that: why some things work their wonder, others do not.

The polyphonal Judaic year follows the lunar calendar, so the appearance of the new moon marks the beginning of a month, and that is celebrated. There are two critical moments in the unfolding of the year, the first full moon after the autumnal equinox, and the first full moon after the vernal equinox. These mark the time of heightened celebration. To understand how the rhythm of the year unfolds, however, we begin with the new moon of the month of Tishri, corresponding to September. That marks the New Year, Rosh Hashanah.

The Days of Awe: Israel before God

Ten days later, as we realize, comes the Day of Atonement, commemorating the rite described in Leviticus 16, and marking God's judgment and forgiveness of humanity. Five days afterward is the full moon, the beginning of the Festival of Tabernacles, or *Sukkot;* this festival lasts for eight days and ends with a day of solemn assembly, *Shemini Aseret,* and of rejoicing of the Torah, *Simhat Torah.* So nearly the whole month of Tishri is spent in celebration: eating, drinking, praying, studying, enjoying and celebrating God's sovereignty, creation, revelation, redemption, as the themes of the festivals and solemn celebrations of the season work themselves out. The next major sequence of celebration, as we realize, follows the first new moon after the vernal equinox, which begins the month of Nisan and culminates, at its full moon, with Passover, or *Pessah,* which commemorates the Exodus of Israel from Egypt and celebrates Israel's freedom, bestowed by God. Fifty days thereafter comes the festival of Pentecost, or *Shavuot,* which commemorates the giving of the Torah at Mount Sinai. Other occasions for celebration exist; but, apart from the Sabbath, as I have said, the New Year, the Day of Atonement, the Feast of Tabernacles, Passover, and Pentecost are the main holy days.

Just as the Days of Awe, the New Year and the Day of Atonement, and the festivals of Tabernacles, Passover, and Pentecost, mark the passage of the lunar year, so the Sabbath marks the movement of time through the week. The sanctification of the Sabbath, observed on the seventh day, Saturday, is in accordance with one of the Ten Commandments. It is the single happiest moment in Judaism, and, coming as it does every week, the Sabbath sheds its light on the everyday. On the Sabbath, as I have described, people do no servile labor and

devote themselves to sacred activities, including both syna-
gogue worship and study of the Torah, as well as to eating,
drinking, relaxing, and enjoying themselves. The song for the
Sabbath day, Psalm 92, expresses the spirit of this observance:
It is good to give thanks to the Lord. Faithful Jews find in the
Sabbath the meaning of their everyday lives.

The passage of the individual's life, from birth to death,
marks out the third of the three joined voices, the cycles that
convey the spirit of the Torah, or law as the word is translated.
The principal points of this cycle are birth, puberty, marriage,
and death. Birth in the case of males is marked by circumcision
on the eighth day. Nowadays in the synagogue the birth of
either a son or a daughter is celebrated by a rite of naming of
the child. When a child becomes responsible to carry out the
religious duties called *mitzvot,* or commandments, he or she
enters the status known as *bar mitzvah* or *bat mitzvah,* respectively—an event that is celebrated in the synagogue in a simple
way. The young woman or man is called to the Torah, which
she or he reads, and the prophetic passage of the day also is read
by the newly responsible young adult. I have already noted the
marriage ceremony; rites of death, as we shall see in chapter
10, involve a clear recognition that God rules and is the true
and just authority over all humanity. The memorial prayer, or
kaddish for mourners, expresses the worshiper's recognition of
God's holiness and dominion and states the hope for the coming of the Messiah. In a few words, these events of celebration
define an individual's life under the law and how one seeks to
live in accord with God's will, which is that Israel live the holy
life in the here and now and await salvation at the end of time.
So much for everything all together and all at once: a remarkably harmonious statement. And that raises the question with
great force: Why, within an integrated and coherent system

such as I have described, do people celebrate one thing and not another?

The issue is not belief or nonbelief. People who can believe that they are really slaves redeemed from Pharaoh in Egypt, who can pretend that they are Adam and Eve in Eden, who are willing to have a piece of a son's penis chopped off on the eighth day after birth—such people will believe anything and do anything. There is nothing more or less compelling in the reason for the Sabbath than the reason for the Passover banquet rite, though, considering the values embedded in the Sabbath, that rite enjoys a more direct relevance to this country and this time than does Passover. If the issue is not that the more reasonable is the more practiced, then what explains the power of some words and not others? In my view, the issue is the question and the answer: people will believe all sorts of things if they want to, and deny the end of their nose if they do not want to.

The rites of the actually practiced Judaism, denoted by the words that create worlds, have in common a single trait: it is their focus on the individual, inclusive of the family. The rites of the Judaism that for the generality of Jewry do not work to make worlds exhibit this common trait: they speak to a whole society, or to civilization, to nation or people. The corporate community, doing things together and all at once, conducts worship (as we shall see in chapter 11) as service. The corporate community celebrates and commemorates events in the world of creation, revelation, and redemption. The Sabbath and the festivals focus upon the corporate life of Israel, a social entity: the words that people say on these occasions speak to but Jews. The individual rites of passage, celebrating family, such as circumcision, marriage, and the rites that focus upon the individual and his or her existence, such as the Days

[109]

of Awe, retain enormous power to move people. What speaks to the family on Passover, the home rite of the banquet, and, moreover, addresses the situation that the individual or family identifies as pertinent, resentment and remission—that component of Passover enjoys nearly universal response. Alongside, the banquet symbol, *matzah,* will impose its spell, so that people who through the year and on Passover do not keep the dietary taboos do give up bread for the week and eat only *matzah.* At the same time, the synagogues on Passover contain plenty of empty seats. In my judgment, therefore, words work to make very private and personal worlds. Words do not work to create a corporate world of all Israel. In this collective denial of the public and the communal, the *we* gives way in favor of the *I,* and that is what accounts for what people do and also for what they ignore.

To do its work, a world has to form an answer to a question people want to ask. Basically, people respond to the answers to questions they find urgent. And then, in general, the substance of an answer will not make much difference to them, so long as its question is addressed. No answer proves more credible or less credible than any other, once its question has been asked. So the question answered by the Passover banquet rite concerns resentment of the gentile, of being a minority, of the sense of difference. The answer transforms difference into destiny—slaves redeemed from Egypt indeed!—but then promises that, at some point, there will be no more differences anyhow. In form, both question and answer are communal and public; but in context, they address the individual in family, at home. Families yes, but no corporate Israel here.

By contrast, the Sabbath and the festivals present powerful answers to the question people do not want to ask. The reason is that, in the stratified life of society, the question proves too personal, the answer too penetrating. Who wishes to be told that what we have does not measure what we are? Not those who have. And yet, in another contrast, the Days of Awe ask a question about *my* life, *my* fate, about what has been and what is coming, that people do find pressing. The Days of Awe form a spell of remission, actually speaking of sin and pronouncing atonement, praying for forgiveness no one seriously imagines will be denied. The mythic language of a God on high, busily writing up each individual among the billions down below, does not provoke amusement but invokes awe, fear, reflection. It is because when people want to ask and answer a question, a deeply mythic mode will serve as well, or as incredibly, as any other. And that is the case even, as here, when the question is personal and private, the answer proves public and communal. Once more, therefore, the question proves the key. If the Sabbath and the festivals address an unwanted answer to an unasked question, we can hardly expect holy days of sin and atonement to gain much entry into Jewry. But the opposite is the case.

Why this, not that? At this stage in the argument, I point to the message contained in the rites that speak to the subjectivity and individuality of circumstance, that lay stress on private person, that recognize and accord priority to the autonomous individual. What people find personally relevant they accept; for them, the words evoke meaning and make worlds. Scarcely heard are the rites that speak to the community out there beyond family, to the corporate existence of people who see themselves as part of a social entity beyond. The context accounts, therefore, for the difference and even for variations. Jews live one by one, family by family. Words that speak to that individuality work wonders. Jews form not a corporate community but only families. Words that address Israel not as a congregation of individual Jews but as a community bound by law to do some things together, fall unheard, mere magic, not wonder working at all.

That larger social context not of belief but of experience tells us which words produce worlds, which do not. For the Jews really do respond to the holy occasions that speak of the individual including the family, while they have difficulty dealing with the ones that address the collectivity of public experience. The enchantment wrought by life in the democratic West should not be overlooked. The *I* even before God remains always the *I,* and the *we* is just that: many *I*'s formed into families—only that, not something more *and something else.* Israel before God is made up of Israelites, individual and family, counted solely one by one, family by family. For the sum of the whole is merely the same as the parts. But it is magic that makes the whole greater than the sum of the parts. In Judaism today, that magic does not work; and the whole is not more, but less, than the sum of the parts.

To state the upshot in secular terms, the fundamental condition of "being Jewish"—so far as people identify "being Jewish" with the received Judaism of the dual Torah—in the West involves individual and family *but imparts in social experience no knowledge of what it means to live in corporate community.* People cannot appeal to experience of a life in Israel and as Israel, an entire social entity, so as to validate the issues resolved by the rites of the .corporate community, the Sabbath, for example, and the synagogue. The questions of community not asked, not felt, not understood, the answers in rite give information no one needs or can use. That is why—to revert to our starting point—the cognitive ordering of the categories of time, space, action, and community in rite takes place when individual imagination participates, and does not take place when the experience of the individual in family as part of a larger social entity can be invoked. The deep can call only to deeps where we have swum or crawled—but not to depths of experience none has plumbed. *As if* depends on *is*.

CHAPTER 8

Jewish Law and Learning: The *Halakhah* and *Talmud Torah*

THE *as if* of *I* and *we* alike become the *is* of Judaism through the transforming power of *halakhah,* norms of behavior or way of life, and through *Talmud Torah,* study of the Torah which is God's statement—that is, revelation—of the divine purpose in creating the world and of His will for Israel. The rules tell how to act so as to change commonplace deed into statement, gesture, therefore metaphor; and Torah study shows how to see the everyday as commemoration, celebration, and simile. In understanding these two fundamental powers within the Judaic framework, we can identify those words that create worlds of deed and deliberation, and also explain why some words do not effect transformation.

Judaic enchantment invokes Jews' power to imagine things as other than what they are, but that power derives, to begin with, from Jews' experience of how things actually are. In the beginning is the world as we know it; and then, out of that, we create, through words, those other worlds. These prove more than and different from the ordinary world, but they also are continuous and consubstantial with the perceived world of the everyday. When, therefore, we point to Jews' power to translate their hunger and satisfaction into the story of exile and redemption, their marvelous capacity to see bride and groom as Eve and Adam in the *huppah* that is an imaginary Eden, and their suspension of incredulity sufficient to draw them to a synagogue service that puts them on trial and declares them at risk of death, we call attention to the strength of imagination to transform. But what is transformed is a component of the human condition: hunger, joy, a sense of the passage of time and life, as captured in the Grace after Meals, the rite of the *huppah,* and the Days of Awe, respectively.

The imagination cannot work its wonder upon a world it has not known. Jews identify with the religious world experiences of the individual in rites of passage and events in the home and family. That is why the social imagination of Jewry engages with Judaism in its narrative of the rites of the passage through life, on the one side, and of a social experience mediating between home and family and the sheltering world, on the other. Circumcision and the Passover-banquet *seder* bear in common a single social referent: family, home, and experiences of essentially private life. Sabbath and festivals (even the morning after the Passover *seder*) and many (though obviously not all) of the other rites presently neglected fail because they invoke in common another social referent: society beyond individual and family. That social world beyond, which people take for granted, has no bearing upon the mythic life created by the enchantment that transforms the routine into the remarkable and tells a tale about deeds that would, otherwise, invoke no past, no future.

Now let me review the large and general statements concerning the life of home and family that people do accept.

When we ask ourselves what turns individual and family into corporate community, the answer presents itself in simple terms: world view and way of life. These take the givens of the social present and change them through norms, *halakhah* or law, as I shall explain, into the gifts of sheltering society. But that is not how people receive family and home; it is the opposite. In Jewry (and not there alone), people experience a cogent social world, one of integrity and inner coherence, beginning and ending with family. The society beyond presents diversities, both within Jewry and without, such that people cannot refer to a cogent religious life (so far as they define religion as personal, not political) beyond family. It is simply not there. Quite to the contrary, the plurality of society in general, the diversity of Jewry in particular, prevent the formation of that sense of corporate existence beyond the individual in family that would lay foundations for a shared experience of transformation, through rites' enchantment, of the given into a gift. As we shall presently notice, there is, to be sure, a corporate experience of being Israel, which yields a cogent system of a wholly political and public character; but that system differs from this and affects another mode of existence than the one perceived to be personal, familial, religious (see chapter 12).

It follows that, within the nurture of the Jewish life, the experience of reality ends with the family. Whatever is beyond is *as if*. The encounter with reality in the undifferentiated society ends with job and home. The community—other than the city in which we live—is "out there." Then we wonder what in the received social experience of Israel, the Jewish people, is supposed to define the condition of the holy Israel, sharing a corporate sacral existence defined by God's rules. The answer to that question leads us from description of the here and now to an account of the world of *ought* formed out of holy books. For I cannot direct the reader's attention to a present world of Judaism in which, for more than a sect but for an entire encompassing society, the enchantment transforms not family alone but polity: a society or community "out there" in its entirety. Neighborhoods or villages, yes; but these form ghettos, made by the decision of people to manufacture a society through self-segregation. When the families of Israel formed, in the aggregate, the corporate and cogent society of all Israel, it was not by choice but by the nature of the polity itself: Jews saw a commonality beyond themselves; they did not think they had invented it, but knew God had decreed it. Today communities take shape because families decide that they should: a community grows by incremental decision, not by divine decree.

This brings us back to the subject of the Judaic way of life and world view, represented by law and learning—in Hebrew, *halakhah*—on the one side, and by *Talmud Torah,* on the other. The *as if* takes over from the *is* when a social group meets two conditions. First, the group conforms to *halakhah,* as I shall explain. Second, the social group reaches into its shared experience and nurtures a transforming vision, a definition of that deeper reality that underlies things that are not what they seem to be. This inquiry in Judaism takes the form of *Talmud Torah,* study of the Torah in a specific, holy way. I consider first the way of life, then the world view.

Halakhah defines. It governs whether or not people want it to: that is, the norms of the group precede individual or family in the definition of the way of life, and the individual or the family does not make decisions except within the consensus of the community formed, from of old, in the *halakhah*. For the community—nation, people, society, however the social entity be called—transcends the individual and the family, coming before, continuing afterward, and dictates the circumstance of enchantment and transformation, lending credibility to what, done by an individual alone, is mere magic.

Accordingly, rules held in common turn individuals and families into a community. Then, but only then, the enchantment of rite transforms the shared experience of the community, asking questions urgent not to individual or family primarily, but to the community first of all: questions of culture and value, of work and leisure; of all all together, for instance. Second, the group expresses its sense of self in a world view formed on a shared imagination, a pretense of *as if* held in common. For the *as if* becomes the *is* only when enough people join in the drama—when the audience is on stage, so to speak. Short of community, a vision of a community held only by radically isolated individuals or by mere aggregates of families frames the perspective of the sect or the commune or the ghetto. All three have in common the defining of the self against the other, a reliance on the outsider to lend credibility to the sect's or the commune's or the ghetto's isolation and fantasy of isolation. With these matters clear, we ask ourselves how, in the circumstance of a corporate society, Judaism spelled out the world view and the way of life in which the corporate, not only the private, rites worked their magic.

The way of life of corporate, holy Israel finds definition in *halakhah,* by which people state (after the fact mostly) those rules that describe the life they lead. In *halakhah* they record the actions that turn one thing into something else: the sexual union of man and woman into a contracted relationship sanctified by Heaven, for example; the preparation of food into the consecration of the meal; or the saying of words into prayer. *Halakhah,* therefore, constitutes the way of life that, prior to and beyond the experience of family, forms of families a corporate, holy community, Israel in God's sight. When people think of law, they ordinarily imagine a religion for bookkeepers, who tote up the good deeds and debit the bad and call the result salvation or damnation, depending on the outcome. But when we speak of life under the *halakhah* law, we mean life in accord with the *halakhah,* the rules and regulations of the holy life. The mythic structure built upon the themes of creation, revelation, and redemption finds expression not only in synagogue liturgy, but especially in concrete, everyday actions or action symbols—that is, deeds that embody and express the fundamental mythic life of the classical Judaic tradition. So far as the formula or incantation is carried by the blessing or prayer, the gesture of enchantment takes form in *halakhah.* Judaism transforms the ordinary into the holy through both, and the rite on the remarkable occasion takes second place behind the ritualization of the everyday and commonplace—that is to say, the sanctification of the ordinary.

The word *halakhah,* as is clear, is normally translated as "law," for the *halakhah* is full of normative, prescriptive rules about what one must do and refrain from doing in every situation of life and at every moment of the day. But since *halakhah* derives from the root *halakh,* which means "go," a better translation would be "way." The *halakhah* is the "way": the *way* man or woman lives life; the *way* man or woman shapes the daily routine into a pattern of sanctity; the *way* man or woman follows the revelation of the Torah and attains redemption. For the Judaic religious encounter, this *way* is absolutely central. Belief without the expression of belief in the workaday world is of limited consequence. In referring to the enchanted world beyond and within the faith or the Torah, the purpose of revelation is to create a kingdom of priests and a holy people. The foundation of that kingdom, or sovereignty, is the rule of God over the lives of humanity. For the Judaic tradition, God rules much as people do—by guiding others on the path of life, not by removing them from the land of living. Creation lies behind; redemption, in the future; Torah is for here and now. To the classical Jew, Torah means revealed law or commandment, accepted by Israel and obeyed from Sinai to the end of days.

The spirit of the Jewish way *(halakhah)* is conveyed in many modes, for law is not divorced from values but rather concretizes human beliefs and ideals. The purpose of the commandments is to show the road to sanctity, the way to God. In a more mundane sense, a fourth-century rabbi has provided a valuable insight:

> Rava said, "When a person is brought in for judgment in the world to come, that person is asked, 'Did you deal in good faith? Did you set aside time for study of Torah? Did you engage in procreation? Did you look forward to salvation? Did you engage in the dialectics of wisdom? Did you look deeply into matters?' "[1]

Rava's interpretation of Scripture—"and there shall be faith in thy times, strength, salvation, wisdom and knowledge" (Isaiah 33:6)—gives us a glimpse into the life of the Jew who followed the way of Torah. The first consideration was ethical: did the Jew conduct affairs faithfully? The second was study of Torah, not at random but every day, systematically, as a discipline of life. Third came the raising of a family, for celibacy and abstinence from sexual life were regarded as sinful; the full use of a woman's and a man's creative powers for the procreation of life was a commandment. Nothing God made was evil. Wholesome conjugal life was a blessing. But, fourth, merely living day by day according to an upright ethic was not sufficient. It is true that people must live by a holy discipline, but the discipline itself was only a means; the end was salvation. Hence the pious people were asked to look forward to salvation, aiming their deed and directing their hearts toward a higher goal. Wisdom and insight: these completed the list, for without them, the way of Torah was a life of mere routine, rather than a constant search for deeper understanding.

The *halakhah* in detail meant to make a main point, and the literature of the *halakhah*, beginning with the Talmud, articulated that point clearly. One formulation of the entire Torah—law and theology alike—is attributed to Hillel, a first-century authority:

> What is hateful to yourself do not do to your fellow-man. That is the whole Torah. All the rest is commentary. Now go and study.[2]

The saying assigned to Hillel was neither the first nor the last to provide a pithy definition of the Torah or Judaism. In the definition attributed to him, we see that, from among many available verses of Scripture, the selected model is Leviticus 19:18: "You shall love your neighbor as yourself: I am the Lord." This commandment summarized everything.

Still a further definition of the purpose of the *halakhah* as it defines the religious duties, or commandments, incumbent on all Jews as corporate Israel, derives from later rabbis of the Talmud. Thus, Simlai expounded:

Six hundred and thirteen commandments were given to Moses, three hundred and sixty-five negative ones, corresponding to the number of the days of the solar year, and two hundred forty-eight positive commandments, corresponding to the parts of man's body.

David came and reduced them to eleven: *A Psalm of David* [Psalm 15]. *Lord, who shall sojourn in thy tabernacle, and who shall dwell in thy holy mountain?* (i) *He who walks uprightly and* (ii) *works righteousness and* (iii) *speaks truth in his heart and* (iv) *has no slander on his tongue and* (v) *does no evil to his fellow and* (vi) *does not take up a reproach against his neighbor,* (vii) *in whose eyes a vile person is despised but* (viii) *honors those who fear the Lord.* (ix) *He swears to his own hurt and changes not.* (x) *He does not lend on interest.* (xi) *He does not take a bribe against the innocent.* . . .

Isaiah came and reduced them to six [Isaiah 33:25–26]: (i) *He who walks righteously and* (ii) *speaks uprightly,* (iii) *he who despises the gain of oppressions,* (iv) *shakes his hand from holding bribes,* (v) *stops his ear from hearing of blood* (vi) *and shuts his eyes from looking upon evil, he shall dwell on high.*

Micah came and reduced them to three [Micah 6:8]: *It has been told you, man, what is good, and what the Lord demands from you,* (i) *only to do justly and* (ii) *to love mercy, and* (iii) *to walk humbly before God.*

Isaiah again came and reduced them to two [Isaiah 56:1]: *Thus says the Lord,* (i) *Keep justice and* (ii) *do righteousness.*

Amos came and reduced them to a single one, as it is said, *For thus says the Lord to the house of Israel. Seek Me and live.*

Habakkuk further came and based them on one, as it is said [Habakkuk 2:4], *But the righteous shall live by his faith.* [3]

This long passage illustrates in both form and substance the essential attributes of definitions of the *halakhah* seen all together, with the Hebrew Bible as the source of authoritative teaching. But the Scriptures are not cited in a slavish, unimaginative way; rather, they are creatively used as the raw material for the rabbi's own insights.

The power of that vision of *as if,* when extended to Scripture, transforms Scripture into the Judaic system at hand. The direction of life under the law—the corporate life of Israel defined in concrete terms—is the search for God; and the good life consists of that search—"The righteous man shall live by his faith"—for, in Hebrew, the word for "faith" is *emunah,* meaning "trust, loyalty, commitment." Thus, what keeps a person alive, what renders the life of the family real and meaningful, is trust in and loyalty to God, to which the holy community, Israel, is called all together and all at once. The appeal to Scripture alerts us to the definitive trait of the framing of the world view embodied by the way of life of the *halakhah*—that is, appeal to Scripture or, in the language of Judaism, to Torah. So as we move from way of life to world view, we remain within the same enchanted circle of the faith: Torah defining way of life; Torah, properly read, framing world view. The way of life transforms action into *mitzvah,* religious deeds done in compliance with God's will, and the world view transforms thought into *Talmud Torah*—that is, Torah study—seeing the workaday world as a metaphor for God's view of matters.

In examining the practice of reforming the *is* into the *as if,* I noted the emphasis upon Torah, study of Torah, interest in finding in the written and the oral parts of the Torah (which we know as the Hebrew Bible and the Mishnah and Talmud, respectively) not merely what is there but what is there for us. That interest forms an entry into the theory behind the transformation of the everyday into the extraordinary. It consists in reading life as a metaphor for a reality beyond, for—in the language of Scripture—seeing humanity as simile for God: "in our image, after our likeness." The power of *halakhah* to transform details of the everyday derives from the authority of the social imagination to reread the everyday into a set of events in the paradigm of Scripture, and also to rewrite Scripture—the Torah—into a series of accounts of the reality with which the everyday is to be compared. So, in stating the way in which, in theory, the shared *as if* of a social world accomplishes its transformation, we turn to the enchantment of Scripture itself. Let me state at the outset the fundamental fact of theory: the process of metamorphosis—of the *as if* reading of both the everyday and Scripture alike—is full, rich, complete. When everything stands for something else, the something else repeatedly turns out to be the nation. And that is the striking and important fact for our inquiry into where enchantment does its work, and where it does not. Scripture, read in this way, speaks to corporate Israel, not to individual or to family; and the *as if* reading of reality transforms not the private person but everyone, including—by the way—individuals, including families.

Reading one thing in terms of something else, one verse in terms of another, the Judaic theologian-exegetes of Scripture systematically adopted for themselves the reality of the Scripture, its history and doctrines. They transformed that history from a sequence of one-time events, leading from one place to some other, into an everpresent mythic world. No longer was there one Moses, one David, one set of happenings of a distinctive and never-to-be-repeated character. Now whatever happens, of which the thinkers propose to take account, must enter and be absorbed into that established and ubiquitous pattern and structure founded in Scripture. It is not that biblical history repeats itself. Rather, biblical history no longer constitutes history at all—that is, history as a story of things that happened once, long ago, and pointed to some one moment in the future. Rather, it becomes an account of things that happen every day—hence, an everpresent mythic world, as I said. In this way the basic trait of history in the salvific framework, its one-timeness and linearity, is reworked into the generative quality of sanctification, its routine and everyday, ongoing reality.

The rabbinic sages mediated between Israel's perceived condition in an uncertain world and Israel's vivid faith in the God who has chosen Israel and revealed the Torah. Faced with an unredeemed world, sages read Scripture as an account of how things are meant to be. To them, things are not what they seem, and that was a judgment made not only about this world but also about Scripture. This world does not testify to God's wish and plan, and Scripture does not record merely the stories and sayings that we read there. This world serves as a metaphor for Scripture's reality, and Scripture provides a metaphor for Israel's as well. Reading one thing in terms of something else, the rabbinic exegetes exhibited a single trait of mind: that things are not what they seem. The verses of Scripture therefore shift from the meanings they convey to the implications they contain, so speaking about something, anything, other than what they seem to be saying. The *as if* frame of mind brought to Scripture renewed Scripture, with the sage seeing everything with fresh eyes. And the result of the new vision was a reimagining of the social world envisioned by the document at hand: I mean, the everyday world of Israel as corporate society.

For the sages proposed a reconstruction of the shared existence of Israel along the lines of the ancient design of Scripture as they read it. What that meant was that, from a sequence of one-time and linear events, everything that happened was turned into a repetition of known and already experienced paradigms—hence, once more, a mythic being. The source and core of the myth, of course, derived from Scripture—Scripture reread, renewed, reconstructed along with the society that revered Scripture. Corporate Israel rejected their world in favor of Scripture's, reliving Scripture's world in their own terms. Scripture dictated the contents of history, laying forth the structures of time, the rules that prevailed and were made known in events. Self-evidently, these same thinkers projected into Scripture's day the realities of their own, turning Moses and David into rabbis, for example. But that is how people think in that mythic, enchanted world in which, to begin with, reality blends with dream, and hope projects onto future and past alike how people want things to be.

This description of the enchantment of Scripture, its transformation of an account of a one-time sequence of events into an all-the-time set of social rules, requires a concrete example. Otherwise the reader will know only in the abstract what is, in fact, a remarkably imaginative and rich, wholly concrete reading of the received holy book. In fact, corporate Israel today finds its everyday and ongoing life today in the narratives and laws of ancient Israel *then*. To show how this works, I shall impose on the reader's patience and provide a sizable account, in detail, of a remarkable rereading in Scripture of one thing in terms of something else, such as we have seen as well in terms of the everyday life. Then at the end I shall propose a theory to explain how and why the power to transform something into something else works. I deal, specifically, with the reading of the book of Leviticus.

When things are never what they seem, a parable or an allegory transforms Scripture. In Hebrew, the reading of Scripture as parable or allegory turns it from what it seems to wish to say to something beyond, beneath the surface; the word for this process is *Midrash*. How the process of study of Torah through *Midrash* exegesis works is shown in the sages' treatment of diverse biblical books. Let one typify the lot of them.

When the Judaic sages came to Leviticus in particular, they accomplished a most remarkable transformation indeed, for they turned a book that focuses upon the all-the-time sanctification of Israel in the eternal cult of the Temple into a picture of the one-time events that yield reliable historical laws pointing toward the salvation of Israel at the end of time. The book of Leviticus, which concerns the sanctification of Israel's priesthood, is therefore turned into a treatise on a subject—salvation and Israel's society as a whole—that scarcely appears within its pages; and thus is changed from one thing to something else.

Precisely how allegory works for sage-exegetes to turn *is* into *as if* emerges in the following passage, which treats the animals that Israel is forbidden to eat as allegories for the rule of the four pagan monarchies—ending, of course, with Rome as worst but also last, to which Israel is subjugated. What we see in Leviticus Rabbah, which came to redaction approximately a generation after Genesis Rabbah, about A.D. 450, is how sages absorb one-time events into their system of classification of regularities and rules: the opposite of one-time events. Allegory serves as an ideal mode of classification, since it allows many things to be transformed into some few, readily classified ones. That is the magic of *Midrash,* meaning exegesis of Scripture in terms of the living metaphor of Israel's everyday life. The passage takes up a proposition, which is then proved through the systematic compilation of lists of facts, against which the proposition is tested and through which it is validated. Let us turn immediately to the relevant passages of Leviticus Rabbah, where we see how the references of Scripture to animals Jews may or may not eat are shown to refer to a deeper reality, which is the living condition of Israel of the day at hand:

A. Moses foresaw what the evil kingdoms would do [to Israel].

B. "The camel, rock badger, and hare" (Deuteronomy 14:7). [Compare: Nevertheless, among those that chew the cud or part the hoof, you shall not eat these: the camel, because it chews the cud but does not part the hoof, is unclean to you. The rock badger, because it chews the cud but does not part the hoof, is unclean to you. And the hare, because it chews the cud but does not part the hoof, is unclean to you, and the pig, because it parts the hoof and is cloven-footed, but does not chew the cud, is unclean to you (Leviticus 11:4–8).]

There follow plays on words, in which the letters that stand for an animal are read with vowels that yield a different word altogether, as in the following:

C. *"The camel"* (GML) refers to Babylonia [in line with the following verse of Scripture: "O daughter of Babylonia, you who are to be devastated!] Happy will be he who requites (GML) you, with what you have done to us" (Psalm 147:8).

D. *"The rock badger"* (Deuteronomy 14:7)—this refers to Media.

E. Rabbis and R. Judah b. R. Simon:

F. Rabbis say, "Just as the rock badger exhibits traits of uncleanness and traits of cleanness, so the kingdom of Media produced both a righteous man and a wicked one."

G. Said R. Judah b. R. Simon, "The last Darius was Esther's son. He was clean on his mother's side and unclean on his father's side."

H. *"The hare"* (Deuteronomy 14:7)—this refers to Greece. The mother of King Ptolemy was named "Hare."

I. *"The pig"* (Deuteronomy 14:7)—this refers to Edom [Rome].

J. Moses made mention of the first three in a single verse and the final one in a verse by itself [(Deuteronomy 14:7, 8)]. Why so?

K. R. Yohanan and R. Simeon b. Laqish:

L. R. Yohanan said, "It is because [the pig] is equivalent to the other three." [That is, Rome outweighs in evil the other three monarchies put together.]

M. And R. Simeon b. Laqish said, "It is because it outweighs them."

N. R. Yohanan objected to R. Simeon b. Laqish, " *'Prophesy, therefore, son of man, clap your hands [and let the sword come down twice, yea thrice]'* (Ezekiel 21:14)."

O. And how does R. Simeon b. Laqish interpret the same passage? He notes that [the threefold sword] is doubled (Ezekiel 21:14).[4]

[129]

The following dwells on the point that only two of the prophets realized how evil Rome would be:

A.   R. Phineas and R. Hilqiah in the name of R. Simon: "Among all the prophets, only two of them revealed [the true evil of Rome], Assaf and Moses.

B.   "Assaf said, *'The pig out of the wood ravages it'* (Psalm 80:14).

C.   "Moses said, *'And the pig, [because it parts the hoof and is cloven-footed but does not chew the cud]'* (Leviticus 11:7).

D.   "Why is [Rome] compared to a pig?

E.   "It is to teach you the following: Just as, when a pig crouches and produces its hooves, it is as if to say, 'See how I am clean [since I have a cloven hoof],' so this evil kingdom takes pride, seizes by violence, and steals, and then gives the appearance of establishing a tribunal for justice."[5]

The task facing the exegete was to make sense of Rome as Christian, to find an appropriate classification for a Rome that was neither pagan nor Israel. To relate any nation to Israel, sages could appeal only to the operative political metaphor that in their minds explained who was Israel—that is, genealogy. A place had to be found for Rome in the family history of Israel, for Christian Rome did, after all, claim to be part of that history and heir to its blessing. Hence Rome was represented, allegorically, by Ishmael, Esau, or Edom—the rejected side of the family of Israel.

Here we have yet another exercise: Rome pretends to be Israel but is not, as the pig pretends to be suitable for Israelite consumption but is not:

A.   Another interpretation [of GRH, "cud," now with reference to GR, "stranger"]:

B.   *"The camel"* (Leviticus 11:4)—this refers to Babylonia.

C.   *"For it chews the cud"* [now: "brings up the stranger"]—for it exalts righteous men: *"And Daniel was in the gate of the king"* (Daniel 2:49).

D.   *"The rock badger"* (Leviticus 11:5)—this refers to Media.

E.   *"For it brings up the stranger"*—for it exalts righteous men: *"Mordecai sat at the gate of the king"* (Esther 2:19).

F.   *"The hare"* (Leviticus 11:6)—this refers to Greece.

G.   *"For it brings up the stranger"*—for it exalts the righteous.

H.   When Alexander of Macedonia saw Simeon the Righteous, he would rise up on his feet. They said to him, "Can't you see the Jew, that you stand up before this Jew?"

I.   He said to them, "When I go forth to battle, I see something like this man's visage, and I conquer."

J.   *"The pig"* (Leviticus 11:7)—this refers to Rome.

K.   *"But it does not bring up the stranger"*—for it does not exalt the righteous.

L.   And it is not enough that it does not exalt them, but it kills them.

M.   That is in line with the following verse of Scripture: *"I was angry with my people; I profaned my heritage; I gave them into your hand, you showed them no mercy; on the aged you made your yoke exceedingly heavy"* (Isaiah 47:6).

N.   This refers to R. Aqiba and his colleagues [who were martyred by Rome].[6]

[131]

The following makes a direct comment on the sequence of empires, leading to the rise of Israel to rule:

A.   Another interpretation [now treating "bring up the cud" (GR) as "bring along in its train" (GRR)].

B.   *"The camel"* (Leviticus 11:4)—this refers to Babylonia.

C.   *"Which brings along in its train"*—for it brought along another kingdom after it.

D.   *"The rock badger"* (Leviticus 11:5)—this refers to Media.

E.   *"Which brings along in its train"*—for it brought along another kingdom after it.

F.   *"The hare"* (Leviticus 11:6)—this refers to Greece.

G.   *"Which brings along in its train"*—for it brought along another kingdom after it.

H.   *"The pig"* (Leviticus 11:7)—this refers to Rome.

I.   *"Which does not bring along in its train"*—for it did not bring along another kingdom after it.

J.   And why is it then called "pig" (HZYR)? For it restores (MHZRT) the crown to the one who truly should have it [namely, Israel, whose dominion will begin when the rule of Rome ends].

K.   That is in line with the following verse of Scripture: *"And saviors will come up on Mount Zion to judge the Mountain of Esau [Rome], and the kingdom will then belong to the Lord"* (Obadiah 1:21).[7]

The concluding comment forms the climax and the goal of the whole: Israel will rule in the end, after Rome.

I now may state very simply how the *is* of the pig becomes the *as if* of the empire, Rome, which, in the time of the framers of Leviticus Rabbah, had gone from pagan to Christian rule. To stand back and consider this vast apocalyptic vision of Israel's history, we first review the message of the construction as a whole. This comes in two parts: first, the explicit; then, the implicit. As to the former, the first claim is that God had told the prophets what would happen to Israel at the hands of the pagan kingdoms, Babylonia, Media, Greece, Rome. These are further represented by Nebuchadnezzar; Haman; Alexander for Greece; Edom or Esau, interchangeably, for Rome. The same vision came from Adam, Abraham, Daniel, and Moses. The same policy toward Israel—oppression, destruction, enslavement, alienation from the true God—emerged from all four.

How does Rome stand out? First, it was made fruitful through the prayer of Isaac in behalf of Esau. Second, Edom is represented by the fourth and final beast. Rome is related through Esau, as Babylonia, Media, and Greece are not. The fourth beast was seen in a vision separate from the first three. It was worst of all and outweighed the rest. Of the apocalyptic animals of Leviticus 11:4–8 to Deuteronomy 14:7—camel, rock badger, hare, and pig—the pig, standing for Rome, again emerges as different from the others and more threatening than the rest. Just as the pig pretends to be a clean beast by showing the cloven hoof, but in fact is unclean, so Rome pretends to be just but in fact governs by thuggery. Edom does not pretend to praise God but only blasphemes; it does not exalt the righteous but kills them. These symbols concede nothing to Christian monotheism and biblicism. Of greatest importance, while all the other beasts bring further ones in their wake, the pig does not: "It does not bring another kingdom after it." It will restore the crown to the one who will truly deserve it, Israel. Esau will be judged by Zion: so Obadiah 1:21.

Now how has the symbolization delivered an implicit message? It is in the treatment of Rome as distinct from, but essentially equivalent to, the former kingdoms. This seems to me a stunning way of saying that the now-Christian empire in no way requires differentiation from its pagan predecessors. Nothing has changed, except matters have gotten worse. Beyond Rome, standing in a straight line with the others, lies the true shift in history—the rule of Israel and the cessation of the dominion of the (pagan) nations. To conclude, Leviticus Rabbah came to closure, it is generally agreed, around A.D. 450: that is, approximately a century after the Roman empire in the East had begun to become Christian, and half a century after the last attempt to rebuild the Temple in Jerusalem had failed—a tumultuous age indeed. Accordingly, we have had the chance to see how distinctive and striking are the ways in which, in the text at hand, the symbols of animals that stand for the four successive empires of humanity, and point toward the messianic time, served for the framers' message. When we see how the exegetes read one thing in terms of something else, we observe in concrete terms that same mode of thought, applied to Scripture, that transforms the bride and groom under the *huppah* into Eve and Adam in Eden. The ultimate enchantment takes the words of Scripture and transforms them into the world of Israel in the here and now—whether the fourth and fifth centuries, facing the crisis of Rome turned Christian, or the twenty-first century, confronting God alone knows what.

Let us return to the question with which I began. How shall we account for this Judaic system which, in practice and in theory, insists that things are not what they seem? A neutral, secular gesture is governed by *halakhah,* and everything is changed into a metaphor for the scriptural reality—a scriptural reality that itself undergoes stunning metamorphosis. In my view, the tasks of the system, in practice and in theory, find definition in the social experience of the group whose life finds form and meaning in the system. In the case at hand, Judaism in any form is going to have to make sense of the uneven and sometimes difficult life of a small group of people always threatened with extinction through cultural assimilation, yet remarkably persistent through the generations. Judaism must help the corporate society to which it addresses its message to secure some sense of that society's continuity and meaningful difference from others, and do so without either understanding or overstating the importance of that difference. Judaism must explain through the message of the faith—Judaism—why the Jews are what they are and not something else. It must narrate and explain, in a context rich in personal significance, the history of the Jewish people.

Judaism must shape and account for the particular social and psychological experience of living the Judaic life—that is, of pursuing human experience in accord with the distinctive teachings and life pattern of Judaism. In the nature of things, the answers are corporate. For the Jews exhibit differences not one by one: such would stand for mere idiosyncracy. Nor do they differ family by family, for the same reason. Family tradition is not a culture. They differ from non-Jews—that is, the rest of the world as a *they;* and the difference always matters, whatever the shifting marks of distinction. That is why Judaic enchantment in practiced *halakhah* and in theoretical viewpoint intends to take effect for corporate—that is, holy—Israel.

A negative indicator now is called for: What chapters of the private life are left outside the range of transformation and remain only what they are? Furthermore, how shall we explain the difference between those moments and the many others that, as we have seen, are subjected to the rereading of reality as metaphor? Here again we may invoke a single theory to explain both why this and also why not that. The challenge at hand derives from two personal experiences—one trivial, the other decisive—never treated as metaphor but always left as stark, unchanged, and therefore uninterpreted reality: puberty and death.

PART III
Reality without Enchantment

CHAPTER 9

The *Bar* (with and without) *Mitzvah*

THE SINGLE most important rite in contemporary North American Judaism is the celebration of puberty—for boys, among the Orthodox; for boys and girls, among Conservative, Reform, and Reconstructionist, which is to say nearly all Jews. Upon reaching the age of puberty (for males, thirteen; for females, twelve or thirteen), a child is called for the first time to the Torah—an event known as *bar* or *bat mitzvah* for male or female, respectively. *Bar* means "son," and *bat,* "daughter," with the sense of being subject to; and *mitzvah* means "commandment."

The matter is very simple. The young person is called to the Torah, recites the blessing required prior to the public proclamation of a passage of the Torah, and reads that passage (or stands as it is read). When the Torah lection of the week has been read, the congregation proceeds to a passage of the prophets. The young person reads that passage for the congregation. That is the rite—no rite at all.

It is no rite simply because nothing is done on this occasion that is not done by others on the same occasion. The young person is treated no differently from others on this Sabbath, or last week, or next week. He or she simply assumes a place within the congregation of adult Jews, is counted for a quorum, and is expected to carry out the religious duties that pertain. The young person is not asked to imagine himself or herself in some mythic state or setting, such as Eden or Sinai or the Jerusalem of the Messiah's time. The family of the young person does not find itself compared to "all Israel," and no stories are told about how the young person and the family re-enact a mythic event such as the Exodus from Egypt. No one is commanded to see himself or herself as if this morning he or she was born, crossed the Red Sea, entered the Promised Land, or did any of those other things that the dual Torah invokes on enchanted occasions of personal transformation.

Indeed, it is, on the whole, a rather bloodless and impersonal transaction, because what changes is merely status in respect to responsibility. Becoming a *bar mitzvah* or a *bat mitzvah* means that one is subject to the requirement of carrying out religious deeds, that one bears responsibility for himself or herself. That simple transaction—coming for the first time as an adult to assume the rights and responsibilities of maturity—forms the single most powerful occasion in the life of the maturing young Jew and his or her family. It is prepared for, celebrated elaborately, looked back upon as a highlight of life. And, as is clear, it is a moment left without enchantment, just as is death (a point I shall consider in the next chapter).

Only upon achieving intelligence and self-consciousness, normally at puberty, is a Jew expected to accept the full privilege of *mitzvah* ("commandment") and to regard himself or herself as *commanded* by God. But that sense of "being commanded" is impersonal and not imposed by the invocation of any myth. The transaction is neutral: it involves affirmation and assent, confirmation and commitment. But there is no bower, no Eden, no family at table reading a received rite. Judaism perceives the commandments as expressions of one's acceptance of the yoke of the kingdom of heaven and submission to God's will. That acceptance cannot be coerced, but requires thoughtful and complete affirmation. The *bar* or *bat mitzvah* is thus assuming for the first time full responsibility before God to keep the commandments. The calling of the young Jew to the Torah, and the conferring upon him or her of the rights of a full member of the community, ratify what has taken place but effect neither a change in status of the individual nor, even less, a significant alteration in the condition of the community.

Why no rites at all for death and puberty? Because—I claim—these are totally individual experiences. Hence, there can be no appeal to "Israel," with its holy life, its world view. The radically isolated individual cannot be Israel. The reason is that the smallest whole unit of an Israel begins with family (or its surrogate)—that is, with a shared past. The newborn boy-child (and, today, synagogue rites encompass the girl-child and the boy-child as well) undergoes the transformation of circumcision, linking him to the increment of Israel. Marriage, too, is a family event, in which holy Israel has a stake in a way that in death it does not. What makes the difference? Puberty marks no change in the makeup of the community, since the child at birth enters the community and never leaves. Puberty marks merely a shift in the status of an individual, who becomes responsible to the community and to its norms, to God and to God's will.

Death, as we shall see in a moment, is left unaffected by the transforming power of enchanted words because, in the most profound sense, words cannot change what has happened, and because, for that same reason, the one who dies dies alone, within the family, while the community, diminished, goes forward unimpaired. The social entity (nation, holy people, community) takes note; communities celebrate puberty and commemorate death; but community is unchanged: it goes on, augmented by *bar mitzvah,* diminished by death, essentially intact. Only one aspect of death comes, within the received Torah, under the aspect of transformation, as we shall see in a moment. Let me first attend to the simpler of the two matters—puberty.

Here, to recapitulate, there is no real rite, because the individual simply adheres to the ongoing community, of which one (a boy specifically through circumcision) is already a part: one's status changes; community does not change as at birth it changes. At the advent of puberty, with the *bar mitzvah* rite for a young man, and the *bat mitzvah* rite for a young woman, the young person is, as I have said, merely called to pronounce the benediction over a portion of the Torah lection in the synagogue and is given the honor of reading the prophetic passage as well.

And yet that is hardly the entire story of the *bar* or *bat mitzvah*—far from it, as anyone who knows Jews realizes. Where in olden times it was not particularly important, today it is a magnificent occasion, celebrated with vigor and enthusiasm by Jews who otherwise do not often find their way to the synagogue on Sabbath mornings, by Jews married to gentiles, by Jews themselves not "barmitzvahed" (as they say), by Jews remote from any and all connection with Jewish organizations, institutions, activities, observances. First, the occasion calls forth dinners and dances, lavish expenditure on an open bar and a huge meal (hence, the standard joke about "too much bar and not enough mitzvah"). Second, and more to the point, many Jews, myself included, find the occasion intensely meaningful, deeply affecting. And that has nothing to do with either the *bar* or—if truth be told—the *mitzvah*. It is something else.

At a *bar* or a *bat mitzvah* a parent thinks not so much of the future as of the past, especially if a grandparent or a parent is deceased; the entire family one has known has assembled, and that is as much the past as the future. I remember how startled I was to realize how deeply moving my firstborn's *bar mitzvah* turned out to be for my wife and myself. I was not prepared for the intense emotion I felt, as profound as that of only three other occasions in my life: the moment my wife said she would marry me; and the few minutes standing at the graveside of my father and, thirteen years later, of my father-in-law, watching their bodies buried in the ground. Union in love, reunion with the dirt—these mark the turnings of life. But a child's *bar* or *bat mitzvah?* And yet other parents I have known have found themselves profoundly moved at some moment in this rather dull rite—as have I, too, in the *bar mitzvah* celebrations of my next two sons and in the *bat mitzvah* celebration of my daughter.

In order to account for these deep feelings, let me recall what I have written elsewhere about the fear that one is the last Jew on earth, the fear—commonplace among Jews on this other side of the murder of the Jews of Europe now called the "Holocaust"—that one is at the end of the line.[1] There is a deep sense, too, in which one's own generation marks a turning, either downward or upward toward an open future. And the choice is made for life every time a *bar* or a *bat mitzvah* is celebrated. For the *bar* or the *bat mitzvah* today celebrates continuity, tests the strength of the chain of generations and confirms its endurance, and demonstrates that parents, grandparents, and great-grandparents (often present these days) are not the end of the line.

We must remember that Jews have no past, since the Jews who perished in Europe included pretty much all of the families of Jews now alive in the West (excluding only those from the Muslim world, where Jews have endured for centuries). Not only so, but if one's family is two or three generations old in America, no one really knows whether there was a family in Europe, there being no past beyond the grandparents or the great-grandparents who immigrated. My grandmother came from somewhere in the northwest Ukraine. She knew what she left behind, and whom she left behind. I never did, and my father never did. He grew up in Beverly, Massachusetts, and had aunts and uncles all over the north shore of Boston, from Peabody and Lynn and Marblehead to Lowell and Haverhill. That was his family: one generation old. On his father's side, he might as well have come from Jupiter. There was no one. So for me, there is one grandmother, and no past; and for my children, there are only two prior generations. This story of one family stands for the tale of many families: no past, prior to the immigrant generation; no past outside of America. The Jews conjure a long history for their people, but no genealogy for themselves. And the *bar* or *bat mitzvah* forms the remedy to that sense of loss and absence. It forms a past, it points toward a future: the newly mature young woman or man is the link; there is continuity, there is hope, it is not all in vain—whatever the "it" stands for. And that really is something to celebrate, and is why, I think, even in the absence of rite, people invent rituals of *bar* or *bat mitzvah* celebration and spend more than they can afford to carry them out.

But there is yet another side to matters. The young boy or girl spends years preparing to participate in the rite. If for the mother and father the occasion evokes deep feelings of closed-off past and unmarked future, for the child it is still more affecting. To explain why, let me tell my own story. When as a boy in West Hartford, Connecticut, I entered seventh grade, my father allowed me to go to afternoon Hebrew classes at a nearby Orthodox synagogue. It was only for that year; after becoming a *bar mitzvah,* the beginning of the year afterward, I worked in my father's newspaper office every afternoon after school, as well as Saturday mornings, through the end of high school. But in that prepubescent year I met, for the first and only time before my mature years, that realm of the Torah that later defined my being. One day, walking to Hebrew class, which I vastly enjoyed, I began to wonder what would happen when my father died, when "my" rabbi died, when I would be the last Jew on earth—I and maybe my best friend, Eddy: "It must not be that way. I shall not let it. I shall become a rabbi." From then to now, a straight line stretched forward: "Let me not be the last Jew on earth. I shall replace my father—be a better Jew than he was. I will know things." And I did. But not what my father knew— different things.

Jews in America, these Jews without a past and without a well-planned future, fear that the Jews are dying out, and do not want that to happen. They do not want to be the last Jews on earth—and that fear, and the hope it represents, comes to full and complete statement in the *bar* or the *bat mitzvah.* Then we know that we, the parents, are not the last Jews on earth. Then we *know.* Why not celebrate? So there is the *mitzvah* and there is the *bar,* and that is what we celebrate. Thus, as we see, an intensely personal and familial occasion forms the center-piece for a wildly popular rite—one for which the Judaism of the dual Torah has supplied no myth, no ritual, no medium of enchantment. But the world, too, enchants; and its hopes and fears transform.

CHAPTER 10

Death: The Silent World of Real Dirt and Ashes

PUBERTY AND DEATH, stages in the life cycle, for different reasons and in different ways do not undergo that metamorphosis that turns a moment from what it merely seems to be into some other reality. In the Judaic transformation of the everyday, puberty and death remain pretty much untouched. In the language I have used, they stand for no *as if* but merely for an *is*. No metaphor from the corporate experience of Israel fetched from beyond the here and now—no Elijah, no Adam and Eve, no slaves in Egypt—enchants the everyday. In death, I die—*I*, not *we*. Nothing intervenes to turn the stark fact into something other than it is: the end of the life of an individual. No Moses, no Elijah, no David come to join the flights of angels that carry me to my rest. When I reach the age of responsibility for carrying out religious duties, I personally become responsible. No Phineas, no freed slaves join in celebration. I am changed; the occasion is not.

That is not to say, in the case of death, there are no rules everywhere applicable. Quite to the contrary, there are ample *halakhot* for death; and today there are customs that dictate what we do, and do not do, to celebrate the coming of the age of responsibility that marks a young man as a *bar mitzvah,* and a young woman as a *bat mitzvah.* The importance of the rules for death and burial impresses people who otherwise observe little or nothing of the *halakhah.* When I was a student at the Jewish Theological Seminary, the one set of rules we had to learn well concerned death and burial, because—as our teacher, Boaz Cohen, told us—these are the ones you will certainly apply. There are rules—but no myth. An event in the cycle of life—whether death or puberty—profoundly affects the individual and the family but is left unchanged.

A review of the rites of death shows us that all things focus upon the individual, his or her condition; and it is, I claim, for that very reason that we invoke no transforming metaphor. At the onset of death, the dying Jew says a confession:

> My God and God of my fathers, accept my prayer. . . .
> Forgive me for all the sins which I have committed in my lifetime. . . .
> Accept my pain and suffering as atonement and forgive my wrongdoing for against you alone have I sinned. . . .
> I acknowledge that my life and recovery depend on You.
> May it be Your will to heal me.
> Yet if You have decreed that I shall die of this affliction,
> May my death atone for all sins and transgressions which I have committed before You.
> Shelter me in the shadow of Your wings.
> Grant me a share in the world to come.

Father of orphans and Guardian of widows, protect my
beloved family. . . .

Into Your hand I commit my soul. You redeem me, O
Lord God of truth.

Hear O Israel, the Lord is our God, the Lord alone.

The Lord He is God.

The Lord He is God.

What is important in the confession in comparison with other
critical rites of passage is its silence, for what the dying person
does not invoke tells us more than what is said. To state matters
very simply, there is not a word before us—excluding only
the final three lines—that cannot be said by any gentile who
believes in God, sin, atonement, judgment, and reconciliation—which is to say, by any Christian or Muslim. The concluding sentences identify the dying person with the holy
community and its faith. But they, too, do not call to witness—to name familiar spirits—the slaves in Egypt, Adam and
Eve, Elijah, or even the divine Judge seated before an open
book and inscribing the fate of each person.

Nor does the *halakhah* require a gesture to suggest otherwise. Everything that is done concerns the corpse. Little invokes that transforming metaphor that makes of a meal a
celebration of freedom; of an out-of-door picnic, a commemoration of Israel's wandering in the wilderness; of a surgical
operation, a mark of eternal loyalty to God engraved in the
flesh. The corpse is carefully washed and always protected. The
body is covered in a white shroud, then laid in a coffin and
buried. Normally burial takes place on the day of death or on
the following day.

The burial rite at the graveside is laconic. The prayers that are said are exceedingly brief. One prayer that is commonly recited is as follows:

> The dust returns to the earth, as it was, but the spirit returns to God, who gave it. May the soul of the deceased be bound up in the bond of life eternal. Send comfort, O Lord, to those who mourn. Grant strength to those whose burden is sorrow.

It is common to intone the prayer *El Male Rahamim,* "O God full of Compassion":

> O God, full of compassion and exalted in the heights, grant perfect peace in your sheltering presence, among the holy and pure, to the soul of the deceased, who has gone to his eternal home. Master of mercy, we beseech you, remember all the worthy and righteous deeds that he performed in the land of the living. May his soul be bound up in the bond of life. The Lord is his portion. May he rest in peace. And let us say, Amen.[1]

The body is placed in the grave. Three pieces of broken pottery are laid on eyes and mouth as signs of their vanity. A handful of dirt from the Land of Israel is laid under the head. The family recites the *kaddish,* an eschatological prayer of sanctification of God's name, a prayer that looks forward to the messianic age and the resurrection of the dead. The prayer expresses the hope that the Messiah will soon come, "speedily, in our days," and that "he who brings harmony to the heavens will make peace on earth." The words of the mourner's *kaddish* exhibit the remarkable trait that they, too, remain silent, appealing to no metaphor, not even referring to death itself. The following is said by the mourners in what was the vernacular when the prayer was composed:

May the great name [of God] be magnified and sanctified in the world which [God] created in accord with his will.
And may his kingdom come in your life and days, and in the life of all the house of Israel, speedily, promptly.
And say, Amen.

The community says:

May the great name be blessed for ever and all eternity.

The mourner continues:

May the holy name of the blessed one be blessed, praised, adorned, exalted, raised up, adorned, raised high, praised,
Yet beyond all of those blessings, songs, praises, words of consolation, which we say in this world.
And say, Amen.

The community says "Amen." Then the mourner continues:

May great peace [descend] from heaven, [and] life for us and for all Israel.
And say, Amen.

The community says "Amen." Now the following, said by the mourner, comes in Hebrew:

[150]

He who makes peace in the heights will make peace
for us and for all Israel.
And say, Amen.*

The community says "Amen."
The family of the deceased as well as the assembled then
shovel dirt onto the body, until the grave is filled. Then two
lines are formed, leading away from the grave, and the mourners all say the following blessing:

May the Omnipresent comfort you among the other
mourners of Zion and Jerusalem.

The appeal to Zion and Jerusalem, of course, refers to the
Temple of old, which people mourn until the coming restoration—thus, a messianic and eschatological reference, the only
one.

The mourners remain at home for a period of seven days
and continue to recite the memorial *kaddish* for eleven months.
The life cycle for the private individual is simple, but for the
individual as part of Israel, God's holy people, it is rich,
absorbing, and encompassing. Life is lived with people, God's
people, in God's service. And yet we discern no appeal to
presences other than God's, no metamorphosis of death into
something more. All things stand for other things, but death
stands for itself.

*Professor Marvin Fox notes: "In discussing the Kaddish it should be noted that
in the rite which is followed in Orthodox circles a special Kaddish is recited at the
bier. In this form emphasis is placed on the hope for resurrection and redemption.
My guess is that if it has been dropped from Reform and Conservative rituals, and
I do not know for certain that it has, it is because the Aramaic is unfamiliar and
might be difficult for the family to read. In any case, it is there as a normal part
of the funeral service" (personal communication, November 1986; reprinted with
permission).

Yet not entirely. For death does diminish the community, and the social entity has a stake in the matter. To state the matter simply, let me ask a question: What will happen when we all die? Will Israel end too? So far as death happens to the individual, the rite takes note of the individual alone. But so far as death presents doubts to the ongoing community, the rite, too, proposes to take up and transform the event: hence, the one aspect in which the received Judaism proposes to treat death as metaphor. Death stands for eternal life, and death invokes the metaphor of the resurrection of the dead. Death is transformed both in deed and in doctrine by the belief in the resurrection, and that belief is tied to the final judgment at which Israel attains its ultimate salvation at the end of time. In that critical detail in which death engages the ongoing community, the corporate community makes its statement, affecting also the individual and the family. Then, and only then, while the dirt is real dirt, the dead body is turned from a mere corpse into more than mortal matter: a metaphor of the life to come.

That is a matter of both deed and doctrine, way of life and world view, or, in our terms, *halakhah* and *Talmud Torah.* Death does not mark the end of life. In God's time, the dead will live again. The resurrection of the dead stands for the thoroughgoing metamorphosis of a this-worldly experience: death stands for the opposite, for life eternal. In *halakhah,* the transformation takes the form of a particular and strict rule against autopsy or any disfiguring of the corpse. The dead will live: therefore, the body must be preserved, so far as it can be, for the coming resurrection. The counterpart in the study of Torah—that is, the component of the world view that comes to the fore—requires us to uncover proof not that the dead will live but that the doctrine of the resurrection of the dead rests upon Scripture: which is to say that that doctrine was revealed by God in the Torah and not merely by reason, let alone human hope or fantasy.

The "metaphorization" of death takes place, as we should expect, in a set of arguments that turn the *is* of death into the *as if* of life eternal, by which, in the received Judaism of the dual Torah, people mean the bodily resurrection of the dead at the end of time. This transformation of the matter is accomplished, as we should expect, through the proving of propositions through *Midrash* exegesis which embodies, in this context, the activity and world view of *Talmud Torah*. In such exercises, the passage will state its question—How do we know on the basis of Scripture that . . . ?—and then will be spelled out the proposition to be tested against the scientific evidence of Scripture. Then Scripture serves to prove that the stated proposition does conform to, and derive from, the Torah. When, therefore, we wish to understand how Judaism proposes to enchant through words and so to transform the common into the extraordinary—that is, to read one thing in light of some other—we have to follow the exegetes as they demonstrate the presence of propositions paramount in the Torah. Allegory and parable in literary form carry out that process of turning what seems to be into a metaphor for what really is, as we shall now see.

At issue is the proposition attached to the paragraph in the Mishnah that states that *all Israelites have a portion in the world to come.* Of concern in that immediate context is the implicit conviction that the dead rise up and live—a conviction that has now to be linked to verses of Scripture. For among those who will not enjoy the resurrection of the dead and eternal life are people who do not find that belief in Scripture. In this way, treating Scripture as allegory once more allows us to sustain a proposition that, other than read as allegory, Scripture is unlikely to validate. In this sense and context, we may conclude that wherever a proof-text is cited for a proposition not explicitly stated in Scripture, the mode of thought that deems said proof-text probative rests upon an allegorical or a parabolic hermeneutic: *this* proves *that,* because *this* really means or stands for *that.*

We begin with the Mishnah paragraph to which the Talmud of Babylonia appends its sustained proofs (of which I give only a sample) that the Torah maintains that the dead are resurrected and live in eternal life. The Mishnah is presented in regular type, and the verses of Scripture in italics.

A.   All Israelites have a share in the world to come,

B.   As it is said, *"Your people also shall be all righteous, they shall inherit the land forever; the branch of my planting, the work of my hands, that I may be glorified"* (Isaiah 60:21).

C.   And these are the ones who have no portion in the world to come:

D.   He who says that the resurrection of the dead is a teaching which does not derive from the Torah, and that the Torah does not come from Heaven; and an Epicurean.[2]

I now take up the systematic exposition of the passage at hand, with stress on the proposition that Scripture indeed sustains the belief in the resurrection of the dead. The reason that one who denies that belief is not resurrected is mere justice: what you do not believe in, you cannot have.

A.   Why all this [that is, why deny the world to come to those listed]?

B.   Such a one denied the resurrection of the dead, therefore he will not have a portion in the resurrection of the dead.

C.   For all the measures [meted out by] the Holy One, blessed be he, are in accord with the principle of measure for measure.

D.   For R. Samuel bar Nahmani said R. Jonathan said, "How do we know that all the measures [meted out by] the Holy One, blessed be he, accord with the principle of measure for measure?

E.   "As it is written, *'Then Elisha said, Hear you the word of the Lord. Thus says the Lord, Tomorrow about this time shall a measure of fine flour be sold for a shekel, and two measures of barley for a shekel in the gates of Samaria'* (2 Kings 7:1).

F.   "And it is written, *'Then a lord on whose hand the king leaned answered the man of God and said, Behold, if the Lord made windows in heaven, might this thing be? And he said, Behold, you shall see it with your eyes, but shall not eat thereof'* (2 Kings 7:2).

G.   "And it is written, *'And so it fell unto him; for the people trod him in the gate and he died'* (2 Kings 7:20)."

H.   But perhaps it was Elisha's curse that made it happen to him, for R. Judah said Rab said, "The curse of a sage, even for nothing, will come about"?

I.   If so, Scripture should have said, "They trod upon him and he died." Why say, *"They trod upon him in the gate"*?

J.   It was that on account of matters pertaining to [the sale of wheat and barley at] the gate [which he had denied, that he died].[3]

The basic notion of divine justice is now established, and we proceed to the case at hand: Scripture's numerous proofs that the dead will rise on judgment day.

A. How, on the basis of the Torah, do we know about the resurrection of the dead?

B. As it is said, *"And you shall give thereof the Lord's offering set aside as the priestly ration to Aaron the priest"* (Numbers 18:28).

C. And will Aaron live forever? And is it not the case that he did not even get to enter the Land of Israel, from the produce of which heave-offering is given?

D. Rather, this teaches that he is destined once more to live, and the Israelites will give him heave-offering.

E. On the basis of this verse, therefore, we see that the resurrection of the dead is a teaching of the Torah.[4]

The first proof for our syllogism sets the model for the rest. We adduce in evidence a verse that presupposes that, at some point in the future, a biblical figure will be alive. Since we know that that person is now dead, we can only surmise that Scripture's implicit syllogism maintains that the dead will rise—or, at least, that person in particular.

We skip some secondary amplification of the foregoing and come directly to the next exercise:

A. It has been taught on Tannaite authority:

B. R. Simai says, "How on the basis of the Torah do we know about the resurrection of the dead?

C. "As it is said, *'And I also have established my covenant with [the patriarchs] to give them the land of Canaan'* (Exodus 6:4).

D.   " 'With you' is not stated, but rather, 'with them,' indicating on the basis of the Torah that there is the resurrection of the dead."[5]

We have the same argument for the same syllogism, merely a different case, proved as the premise of argument requires, by scriptural evidence:

A.   *Minim* [Jewish heretics, sometimes thought to be Jewish–Christians] asked Rabban Gamaliel, "How do we know that the Holy One, blessed be he, will resurrect the dead?"

B.   He said to them [directing their attention to Scripture in particular, rather than to arguments based on natural philosophy], "It is proved from the Torah, from the Prophets, and from the Writings." But they did not accept his proofs.

C.   "From the Torah: for it is written, *'And the Lord said to Moses, Behold, you shall sleep with your fathers and rise up'* (Deuteronomy 31:16)."

D.   They said to him, "But perhaps the sense of the passage is, *'And the people will rise up'*?"

E.   "From the Prophets: as it is written, *'Thy dead men shall live, together with my dead body they shall arise. Awake and sing, you that live in the dust, for your dew is as the dew of herbs, and the earth shall cast out its dead'* (Isaiah 26:19)."

F.   "But perhaps that refers to the dead whom Ezekiel raised up."

G.   "From the Writings, as it is written, *'And the roof of your mouth, like the best wine of my beloved, that goes down sweetly, causing the lips of those who are asleep to speak'* (Song of Solomon 7:9)."

H.   "But perhaps this means that the dead will move their lips?"

I.   That would accord with the view of R. Yohanan.

J.   For R. Yohanan said in the name of R. Simeon b. Yehosedeq, "Any authority in whose name a law is stated in this world moves his lips in the grave,

K.   "as it is said, *'Causing the lips of those that are asleep to speak.'* "

L.   [The *minim* would not concur in Gamaliel's view] until he cited for them the following verse: " *'Which the Lord swore to your fathers to give to them'* (Deuteronomy 11:21)—to them and not to you, so proving from the Torah that the dead will live."

M.   And there are those who say that it was the following verse that he cited to them: " *'But you who cleaved to the Lord your God are alive, everyone of you this day'* (Deuteronomy 4:4). Just as on this day all of you are alive, so in the world to come all of you will live."[6]

The more systematic proof derives from all three divisions of Scripture, and the narrative setting underlines the contentious character of the proposition. The notion that *Midrash* exegesis rests on allegory in the deepest sense—finding in Scripture something that is not explicitly stated but is in the profound layers of Scripture's meaning—is illustrated time and again. We note that the outsider does not ask the question before us, which is the scriptural basis for the belief, but the sage always draws upon verses of Scripture to prove the point. The same phenomenon follows: the Romans or the Aramaeans (the manuscript evidence is never firm on this point) ask Joshua a question in general terms—"How do we know?"—and he answers, "Because Scripture says." In that humble exchange lies the center and heart of rabbinic *Midrash* exegesis: all knowledge derives from or can be shown implicit in Scripture.

>   A.   Romans asked R. Joshua b. Hananiah, "How do we know that the Holy One will bring the dead to life and also that he knows what is going to happen in the future?"
>   B.   He said to them, "Both propositions derive from the following verse of Scripture:
>   C.   "As it is said, '*And the Lord said to Moses, Behold you shall sleep with your fathers and rise up again, and this people shall go awhoring . . .*' (Deuteronomy 31:16)."
>   D.   "But perhaps the sense is, '[the people] will rise up and go awhoring.' "
>   E.   He said to them, "Then you have gained half of the matter, that God knows what is going to happen in the future."[7]

This exchange is, for the outsider, somewhat unsatisfying, since the sage does not complete the required proof. But the insider understands that he has given a fine and solid answer. And if we were to miss that point, precisely the same answer to the correctly framed question is now repeated:

>   A.   It has also been stated on Amoraic authority:
>   B.   Said R. Yohanan in the name of R. Simeon b. Yohai, "How do we know that the Holy One, blessed be he, will bring the dead to life and knows what is going to happen in the future?
>   C.   "As it is said, '*Behold, you shall sleep with your fathers, and . . . rise again . . .*' (Deuteronomy 31:16)."[8]

We cannot miss the simple point that Joshua's proof-text serves quite well, despite this unsatisfactory conclusion.

A. It has been taught on Tannaite authority:

B. Said R. Eliezer b. R. Yose, "In this matter I proved false the books of the *Minim*.

C. "For they would say, 'The principle of the resurrection of the dead does not derive from the Torah.'

D. "I said to them, 'You have forged your Torah and have gained nothing on that account.

E. " 'For you say, "The principle of the resurrection of the dead does not derive from the Torah."

F. " 'Lo, Scripture says, "[*Because he has despised the Lord of the Lord . . .*] *that soul shall be cut off completely, his iniquity shall be upon him*" (Numbers 15:31).

G. " ' ". . . *shall be utterly cut off . . . ,*" in this world, in which case, at what point will ". . . *his iniquity be upon him . . .*"?

H. " 'Will it not be in the world to come?' "

I. Said R. Pappa to Abayye, "And might one not have replied to them that the words 'utterly . . .' '. . . cut off . . . ,' signify the two worlds [this and the next]?"

J. [He said to him,] "They would have answered, 'The Torah speaks in human language [and the doubling of the verb carries no meaning beyond its normal sense].' "

A. This accords with the following Tannaite dispute:

B. " '*That soul shall be utterly cut off*'—'*shall be cut off*' —in this world, '*utterly*'—in the world to come," the words of R. Aqiba.

C. Said R. Ishmael to him, "And has it not been said,

'He reproaches the Lord, and that soul shall be cut off' (Numbers 15:31). Does this mean that there are three worlds?

D. "Rather: *'. . . it will be cut off . . . ,'* in this world, *'. . . utterly . . . ,'* in the world to come, and *'utterly cut off . . . ,'* indicates that the Torah speaks in ordinary human language."

E. Whether from the view of R. Ishmael or of R. Aqiba, what is the meaning of the phrase, "His iniquity shall be upon him"?

F. It accords with that which has been taught on Tannaite authority:

G. Is it possible that that is the case even if he repented?

H. Scripture states, *"His iniquity shall be upon him."*

I. I have made the statement at hand only for a case in which "his iniquity is yet upon him" [but not if he repents].[9]

The next corollary requires that we treat the resurrection in the context not of scriptural proof but of topical rationality. It is simply rational to maintain that the dead will live. Scripture confirms the fact that reason proposes:

A. A Tannaite authority of the house of R. Ishmael [taught], "[Resurrection] is a matter of an argument *a fortiori* based on the case of a glass utensil.

B. "Now if glassware, which is the work of the breath of a mortal man, when broken, can be repaired,

C. "A mortal man, who is made by the breath of the Holy One, blessed be he, how much the more so [that he can be repaired, in the resurrection of the dead]."[10]

We conclude with controversy stories, between sages and *minim,* or Jewish heretics, on the question at hand. Familiar themes now recur within a fresh setting:

A.   A *min* said to R. Ammi, "You say that the dead will live. But they are dust, and will the dust live?"

B.   He said to him, "I shall draw a parable for you. To what may the matter be compared?

C.   "It may be compared to the case of a mortal king, who said to his staff, 'Go and build a great palace for me, in a place in which there is no water or dirt [for bricks].'

D.   "They went and built it, but after a while it collapsed.

E.   "He said to them, 'Go and rebuild it in a place in which there are dirt and water [for bricks].'

F.   "They said to him, 'We cannot do so.'

G.   "He became angry with them and said to them, 'In a place in which there is neither water nor dirt you were able to build, and now in a place in which there are water and dirt, how much the more so [should you be able to build it]!'

H.   "And if you [the *min*] do not believe it, go to a valley and look at a rat, which today is half-flesh and half-dirt and tomorrow will turn into a creeping thing, made all of flesh. Will you say that it takes much time? Then go up to a mountain and see that today there is only one snail, but tomorrow it will rain and the whole of it will be filled with snails."[11]

In this protracted exercise, we see in detail how the intellect has composed an infrastructure of reasoned syllogistic argument in behalf of the proposition and practice represented by belief in the resurrection of the dead. The practice that forbids autopsy is a concrete expression of the proposition that death is a metaphor.

And the two, proposition and practice, coalesce in the conviction that Israel, the holy nation or people or community, transcends death. That conviction accounts for the power, for those who believe, of *halakhah* and *Talmud Torah* alike to treat the naked corpse as a sign of the coming life, the stark moment of death as the ultimate metaphor. Time at the grave, invoking God's kingdom and rule, is reordered into end-time; the space is not the here and now but God's kingdom; the action is not mere burial but preparation for renewal; and the community—that remains always and everywhere not merely you and I, the *we* of family and friends, but the *we* of all Israel, represented in the here and now by you and me.

PART IV
Enchantment and Transformation: What We Do Together

CHAPTER 11

The World of the Synagogue

NOW that we have begun to form a theory of where and why words work and do not work, we confront the single most puzzling fact in contemporary Judaism. It is the contrast between the vivid and encompassing life of the faith in families, and the decadent state of the synagogue in its critical function, which is the offering up of prayer day by day and on Sabbaths and festivals. The simple fact that families covering nearly the whole of American Israel celebrate the Passover banquet *seder,* but only paltry numbers then assemble the next morning in synagogue worship, states the question. The fact that nearly all Jews bury their deceased in accord with the rites of Judaism (whether Reform or Orthodox) underlines the question. Why the one, not the other? My answer comes in two parts: first, Jews fundamentally misunderstand the nature and meaning of public worship in Judaism; second, public worship rests upon the experience of the corporate community, which is responsible *in the aggregate* for offering up prayers. But any common experience of the world Jews as a whole confess to bears no relationship to worship or the responsibilities of divine service. So, once more, Judaism becomes an exercise, by choice, of home and family, rather than an expression, out of duty imposed from above and beyond, of the corporate community, Israel God's people. People who do not in their ordinary life experience the commonality of community fail also, in their cultic life, to conceive that a task awaits for which all bear responsibility, and to which prove immaterial the personal attitudes and feelings of the individual.

The conception of prayer characteristic of the Judaism of the dual Torah, which took shape in the first six centuries of the Common Era and predominated from then to now, derives from the Temple and its priesthood and offerings. Prayer, that Judaism held, continues the offerings of the altar to God. Now the priesthood in the book of Leviticus represented those offerings in a very particular way, and that representation predominates in the Mishnah, *c.* 200, and in its exegetical continuations in the Tosefta, the Talmud of the Land of Israel, and the Talmud of Babylonia, *c.* 300–600. In these definitive documents, the priestly conception of the Temple cult shaped the synagogue activity of prayer. That conception treated the offerings of the altar in the Temple in Jerusalem (the "tent of meeting" of the books of Exodus, Leviticus, and Numbers) as responses to God's command: This you shall do. The language is simple: "The Lord spoke to Moses saying, Speak to the children of Israel and say to them. . . ." The command addressed the community as a whole through the priesthood.

Specifically, the community of Israel was to offer on the altar a daily whole-offering, dawn and dusk; and the obligation of that whole-offering rested on the holy people as a whole. The Mishnah carried forward that conception in its definition of the half-shekel offering that every Jew was to pay to the Temple as one's personal share in the corporate cost of the everyday whole-offerings. The half-shekel from each man—no more, no less—was owing, since the obligation rested on each one. Then the priests acted in behalf of Israel as a whole, carrying out the public and common obligation.

Scripture contained other conceptions of prayer, but none of divine service. Scriptural books most certainly recognize personal prayer of petition and intercession. Hannah's prayer in 1 Samuel 2:1, "My heart exults in the Lord, I have triumphed through the Lord. . . . I rejoice in your deliverance"; the meditations of Jeremiah; the numerous personal prayers in Psalms (for example, "The Lord is my shepherd, I shall not want")—all of these testify to the broad recognition that prayer as such spoke for the individual. The cult, for its part, made equal provision for individual offerings: for example, sin offerings to expiate unwitting sin, guilt offerings, free-will offerings, thank offerings, and peace offerings. But the community owed the daily whole-offering and its Sabbath and festival counterparts; and, by that analogy, obligatory prayer was incumbent in particular upon the corporate community of holy Israel.

Since what the community owed, which the individual did not, were regular and routine public offerings, public prayer —in the aftermath of the destruction of the Temple—took the place of these offerings and was owing from the community just as offerings were. (That is not to suggest that, prior to the end of the animal sacrifices with the destruction of the Temple in Jerusalem in 70, such a conception did not characterize public worship; the issue is not germane to my argument.) One example of that prevailing conception derives from the debates in the Talmud about whether the recitation of a certain prayer is valid even when done mechanically and not devoutly. The prayer, the recitation of the *Shema,* which I shall review in a moment, does not contain personal requests but reviews certain passages of Scripture. The recitation of these scriptural passages functions as a creed in the context of public worship. At issue is whether, when one recites the verses of Scripture that constitute the prayer, the *Shema,* one is fulfilling the obligation to recite the creed if one says the words without what is called *kavvanah,* which means reflection and proper intention. Specifically, if I simply mumble the words without feeling in them any personal meaning, if I merely go through the motions, does that count?

Now when I was a student at the Jewish Theological Seminary of America, intent on something I then called spirituality (which I can no longer define in the terms of Judaism at all), I cheered for the side that argues that merely repeating the words without feeling or engagement does not count. What could be more obvious than that prayer without engagement was mere words? But, in the present context, I recognize what I did not grasp then: that is, the simple fact that, once prayer becomes incumbent on the community at large, then the fulfilling of the obligation—properly reciting the words—is what matters: that alone. True, proper engagement is praiseworthy. But the rite, done right, suffices. The Temple offerings (again invoking the priestly analogy for public worship, which is the only available metaphor in Judaism) did not require that the priest express appropriate *kavvanah,* intention stated in words. Quite to the contrary, the cult was carried out in perfect silence—lest the priest express the wrong intention! And excluding the opening line, the *Shema,* too, is said silently—and so, too, the Prayer of Supplication, the Eighteen Benedictions, to which I shall turn shortly as well. The corporate community is just that: everyone acting all at once. To the works of such a community, the attitude of the individual is irrelevant. A further example of that same fact derives from

[170]

the *Mussaf,* or additional service, added to the worship, within the received liturgy, of Sabbaths and festivals. That service corresponds to the additional offering required on those same occasions in the Temple, a kind of extra meal in celebration of the holy day. An individual praying all alone may, strictly speaking, omit that prayer, although the community is obligated in public worship to recite it. The community as such does the task, bears the responsibility, enjoys the benefit. God wants us all, as a community, to do certain things; and, among them, is the labor of reciting the right words at the right time.

The conception that liturgy forms a labor in service of God that *we* must do, whether we wish to do it or do not, will not strike as alien at least some Christian communions. I may translate it into the issue of whether the priestly ordination depends upon the character of the ordained or is indelible; the view that a sinful priest cannot offer the Eucharist devastated the Church of North Africa in the aftermath of priestly apostasy under persecution, followed by return in conditions of remission. But the notion, rejected by some such as the Donatists, of the indelibility of the priestly calling held sway. The work did not depend upon the attitude or even the character of the priest, but upon the proper conduct of the rite: that alone. When Roman Catholic and Orthodox churches undertake the liturgy of reciting prayers in the conviction that the saying of those words bears sacred value and not only personal meaning, the same fundamental conception of public prayer as communal obligation pertains.

That conception of public worship as obligatory, owing quite independent of the feelings and attitudes of the private individual, contradicts a common view, characteristic of one wing of Protestant communions but not of the apostolic, historical, and Reformation Protestant churches, on the one side, or of the Roman Catholic or Orthodox churches, on the other. It is the view that prayer is personal, expresses deepest emotions validated (or invalidated) within the individual heart, and is not primarily public, though people may do it together. God calls to each, and the individual responds to the call, each one, one by one. Prayer takes place not as public performance of duty—recitation in common of the required words, sacrifice for the community at large, the carrying out of objective obligations—but responds to the heart and is the outpouring of the heart: therefore, prayer starts in private and only then is shared. This conception of prayer is the opposite of an obligation incumbent on the community, in that the community hardly forms a significant component of the transaction—except after the fact. Within this conception, prayer is something that individuals do by themselves and that they feel; it is not duty but grace, not obligatory but optional in the deepest sense. Specifically, prayer, when possible, constitutes the human response to grace. From this point of view, mechanically saying the words—whether of the "Hail Mary," or of the "Our Father," or the *Shema* that says "Hear, O Israel"—makes no difference in heaven or on earth. But the priests of the ancient Temple and their continuators, the rabbis of the Mishnah and the Talmud and down to our own time, see prayer as public and communal. The premise is that corporate society bears obligations to heaven, a part of which society as a whole carries out by saying the right words and making the right gestures.

People with no knowledge of a religious life lived out in corporate society, who see religion as, if not utterly personal, then fundamentally familial, can hardly expect themselves to recognize obligations to offer up, as a group, the recitation of certain words. The issue is not that offering up unfelt words taxes the imagination, while offering up compelling words makes sense. The same social experience that tells us why the vast majority of Jews form families to observe the Passover banquet rite explains why they do not ordinarily participate in public worship in the synagogue. Their social experience informs them that, under the aspect of eternity, to be a Jew is to be part of a family, but tells them little in the aspect of their inner life about corporate responsibilities as a community. (I am not suggesting that they do not form a corporate community; in politics, in history, in society, even in economics, they do. But the realm of the sacred—that is, what they understand by "religion"—touches their passage through life and draws them into contact with others principally through home and family, as I shall argue in chapter 12.)

Some words evoke worlds, others do not, because some words refer to worlds we know, others speak of things we cannot recognize or identify. The individual in family understands life as metaphor. The family as part of community within the realm of religion does not. Corporate Israel exists in other dimensions, but not in the religious one. Consequently, the synagogue, which has served the specific purpose of divine service to God through both the provision of public worship (as is required of the community) and the study of the Torah in public (as is also demanded of the community), both changes and decays. It changes into a community center, flourishing (where it does) in those aspects of its program to which the holy words scarcely reach. It decays in that the service of the heart becomes lip-service, words passively mumbled in suppression of utter incredulity. And that brings us to the words themselves.

[173]

The recitation of public prayers, obligatory on the community (as well as on the individual), encompasses three important matters: recitation of the creed, petition for the needs and welfare of the community and the individual, and the situation or identification of the community in its larger setting. Accordingly, we find ourselves on a tour through the world that Judaism composes for Israel: world view, way of life, larger theory of who is Israel. I cannot imagine a more systematic or orderly exposition of that enchanted world precipitated by the recitation of the right words in the right way at the right time. The *Shema* ("Hear, O Israel, the Lord our God, the Lord is one") presents the creed, hence the view of the world in its entirety. The Prayer of Supplication, or Eighteen Benedictions (Hebrew, *Shemoneh esré*), covers the everyday needs of the community viewed in its own terms. The concluding prayer, *Alenu* ("It is our duty . . ."), a prayer of departing for the world, then states the theory of Israel to which the world view of the *Shema* and the way of life outlined in the Eighteen Benedictions refer.

Evening and morning, Israel individually and communally proclaims the unity and uniqueness of God. The proclamation is preceded and followed by blessings. The whole constitutes the credo of the Judaic tradition. It is "what the Jews believe." Components recur everywhere. The three elements of the creed cover creation, revelation, and redemption: that is to say, God as creator of the world, God as revealer of the Torah, God as redeemer of Israel. The recital of the *Shema* is introduced by a celebration of God as creator of the world.

Creation of the World, attested by sunrise, sunset

In the morning, the individual, in community or not, recites these preliminary benedictions:

Praised are You, O Lord our God, King of the universe.
You fix the cycles of light and darkness;
You ordain the order of all creation;
You cause light to shine over the earth;
Your radiant mercy is upon its inhabitants.
In Your goodness the work of creation
Is continually renewed day by day.

. . . .

O cause a new light to shine on Zion;
May we all soon be worthy to behold its radiance.
Praised are You, O Lord, Creator of the heavenly
bodies.

The corresponding prayer in the evening refers to the setting of the sun:

Praised are You. . . .
Your command brings on the dusk of evening.
Your wisdom opens the gates of heaven to a new day.
With understanding You order the cycles of time;
Your will determines the succession of seasons;
You order the stars in their heavenly courses.
You create day, and You create night,
Rolling away light before darkness. . . .
Praised are You, O Lord, for the evening dusk.

Morning and evening, Israel responds to the natural order of the world with thanks and praise of God who created the world and who actively guides the daily events of nature. Whatever happens in nature gives testimony to the sovereignty of the creator. And that testimony is not in unnatural disasters but in the most ordinary events: sunrise and sunset. These, especially, evoke the religious response to set the stage for what follows.

For Israel God is not merely creator but purposeful creator. The works of creation serve to justify and to testify to Torah, the revelation of Sinai. Torah is the mark not merely of divine sovereignty but of divine grace and love, source of life here and now and in eternity. So goes the second blessing:

Revelation of the Torah, as the expression of God's love for Israel

Deep is Your love for us, O Lord our God;
Bounteous is Your compassion and tenderness.
You taught our fathers the laws of life,
And they trusted in You, Father and king,
For their sake be gracious to us, and teach us,
That we may learn Your laws and trust in You.
Father, merciful Father, have compassion upon us:
Endow us with discernment and understanding.
Grant us the will to study Your Torah,
To heed its words and to teach its precepts. . . .
Enlighten our eyes in Your Torah,
Open our hearts to Your commandments. . . .
Unite our thoughts with singleness of purpose
To hold You in reverence and in love. . . .
You have drawn us close to You;
We praise You and thank You in truth.
With love do we thankfully proclaim Your unity.
And praise You who chose Your people Israel in love.

[176]

Here is the way in which revelation takes concrete and specific form in the Judaic tradition: God, the creator, revealed His will for creation through the Torah, given to Israel His people. That Torah contains the "laws of life."

Moved to worship by the daily miracle of sunrise and sunset, corporate Israel responds with the prayer that Israel, like nature, may enjoy divine compassion. But what does that compassion consist of? The ability to understand and the will to study Torah! This is the mark of the relationship between God and the human being—the Jewish person in particular: that a person's eyes are open to Torah; and a person's heart, to the commandments. These are the means of divine service and of reverence and love for God. Israel sees itself as "chosen"—close to God—because of Torah, and finds in its devotion to Torah the marks of its chosenness. The covenant made at Sinai—a contract on Israel's side to do and hear the Torah; on God's side, to be the God of Israel —is evoked by natural events and then confirmed by the deeds and devotion of corporate Israel. The corporate framework of the public prayers is implicit everywhere and explicit in the recurrent *we*. We look in vain for the private person. What we see instead is the community affirming its obligation, carrying out its duty. In this context, those rites of passage upon which, nowadays, people focus with such intent appear trivial and personal, forming a stunning contrast to the majestic and public concern for the entirety of the cosmos and all of life.

In the *Shema*, Torah—revelation—leads Israel to enunciate the chief teaching of revelation:

Hear, O Israel, the Lord Our God, the Lord is One.

This proclamation of the *Shema* is followed by three scriptural passages. The first is Deuteronomy 6:5–9:

> You shall love the Lord your God with all your heart, with all your soul, with all your might.

And further, one must diligently teach one's children these words and talk of them everywhere and always, and place them on one's forehead and arm, on doorposts and gates. The second Scripture is Deuteronomy 11:13–21, which emphasizes that, if Jews keep the commandments, they will enjoy worldly blessings; but that, if they do not, they will be punished and disappear from the good land God gives them. The third is Numbers 15:37–41, the commandment to wear fringes on the corners of one's garments. These fringes—which are today attached to the prayer shawl worn at morning services by Conservative and Reform Jews and to a separate undergarment worn for the same purpose by Orthodox Jews—remind the Jew of *all* the commandments of the Lord.

The proclamation is completed and yet remains open; for, having created humanity and revealed His will, God is not unaware of events since Sinai. Humanity is frail; and in the contest between the word of God and the will of humanity, Torah is not always the victor. We inevitably fall short of what is asked of us, and Jews know that their own history consists of divine punishment for human failure time and again. The theme of redemption, therefore, is introduced. Redemption—in addition to creation and revelation, the third element in the tripartite world view—resolves the tension between what we are told to do and what we are able actually to accomplish. In the end it is the theme of God, not as Creator or Revealer, but God as Redeemer that concludes the twice-daily drama:

Redemption of Israel then and in the future

You are our King and our father's King,
Our redeemer and our father's redeemer.
You are our creator. . . .
You have ever been our redeemer and deliverer.
There can be no God but You. . . .
You, O Lord our God, rescued us from Egypt;
You redeemed us from the house of bondage. . . .
You split apart the waters of the Red Sea,
The faithful you rescued, the wicked drowned. . . .
Then Your beloved sang hymns of thanksgiving. . . .
They acclaimed the King, God on high,
Great and awesome source of all blessings,
The everliving God, exalted in his majesty.
He humbles the proud and raises the lowly;
He helps the needy and answers His people's call. . . .
Then Moses and all the children of Israel
Sang with great joy this song to the Lord:
Who is like You, O Lord, among the mighty?
Who is like You, so glorious in holiness?
So wondrous your deeds, so worthy of praise!
The redeemed sang a new song to You;
They sang in chorus at the shore of the sea,
Acclaiming Your sovereignty with thanksgiving:
The Lord shall reign for ever and ever.
Rock of Israel, arise to Israel's defense!
Fulfill Your promise to deliver Judah and Israel.
Our redeemer is the Holy One of Israel,

The Lord of hosts is His name.
Praised are You, O Lord, redeemer of Israel.

Redemption is both in the past and in the future. That God
not only creates but also redeems is attested by the redemption
from Egyptian bondage. The congregation repeats the exultant
song of Moses and the people at the Red Sea, not as scholars
making a learned allusion but as participants in the salvation
of old and of time to come. Then the people turn to the future
and ask that Israel once more be redeemed. But redemption is
not only past and future. When the needy are helped, when
the proud are humbled and the lowly are raised—in such
commonplace, daily events redemption is already present. Just
as creation is not only in the beginning but happens every day,
morning and night, so redemption is not only at the Red Sea
but every day, in humble events. Just as revelation was not at
Sinai alone but takes place whenever people study Torah,
whenever God opens their hearts to the commandments, so
redemption and creation are daily events. We note once more
that, while the individual may recite these prayers, the affirmation concerns the entire social entity, holy Israel.

The great cosmic events of creation in the beginning, redemption at the Red Sea, and revelation at Sinai—these are
everywhere, every day near at hand. Israel views secular reality
under the aspect of eternal, ever recurrent events. What happens to Israel and to the world, whether good or evil, falls into
the pattern revealed of old and made manifest each day. Historical events produce a framework in which future events
will find a place and by which they will be understood.
Nothing that happens cannot be subsumed by the paradigm.

Creation, the Exodus from Egypt, and the revelation of

Torah at Sinai are commemorated and celebrated, not merely to tell the story of what once was and is no more, but rather to re-create out of the raw materials of everyday life the "true being"—life as it was, always is, and will be forever. At prayer Israel repeatedly refers to the crucial elements of its corporate being, thus uncovering the sacred both in nature and in history. What happens in the proclamation of the *Shema* is that the particular events of creation—sunset, sunrise—evoke in response the celebration of the power and the love of God, of His justice and mercy, and of revelation and redemption.

The immense statement of the creed in the *Shema* gives way to the second of the three required components of obligatory public worship; that is, prayers of petition, or supplication, which directly address God with requests. What the community asks for—always in the plural—concerns the public welfare and covers matters we should today assign to the category of public policy as much as of personal need. In the morning, noon, and evening, these weekday prayers of petition comprise the Eighteen Benedictions. Some of these, in particular those at the beginning and the end, recur in Sabbath and festival prayers.

The prayer of petition is said silently. Each individual prays by and for himself or herself, but together with other silent, praying individuals. The Eighteen Benedictions are then repeated aloud by the prayer leader, for the prayer is both private and public, individual and collective. To contemplate the power of these prayers, imagine a room full of people, all standing by themselves yet in close proximity, some swaying this way and that, all addressing themselves directly and intimately to God in a whisper or in a low tone. They do not move their feet, for they are now standing before the King of kings, and it is not meet to shift and shuffle. If spoken to, they will not answer. Their attention is fixed upon the words of supplication, praise, and gratitude. When they begin, they bend their knees—so, too, toward the end; and at the conclusion, they step back and withdraw from the Presence. These, on ordinary days, are the words they say. The introductory three paragraphs define the One to whom petition is addressed: (1) the God of the founders, who is (2) omnipotent and (3) holy. The text of the three opening benedictions follows:

The Founders

Praised are you, Lord our God and God of our fathers, God of Abraham, God of Isaac, and God of Jacob, great, mighty, revered God, exalted, who bestows lovingkindness and is master of all things, who remembers the acts of loyalty of the founders and who in love will bring a redeemer to their descendants for his great name's sake. King, helper, savior and shield, praised are you, Lord, shield of Abraham.

God's Power

You are powerful forever, Lord, giving life to the dead. You are great in acts of salvation. You sustain the living in loyalty and bring the dead to life in great mercy, holding up the falling, healing the sick, freeing the prisoners, and keeping faith with those who sleep in the dirt. Who is like you, Almighty, and who is compared to you, King who kills and gives life and brings salvation to spring up? And you are reliable to give life to the dead. Praised are you, Lord, who gives life to the dead.

God's Sanctity

We shall sanctify your name in the world just as they sanctify it in the heights of heaven. . . . Holy, holy, holy is the Lord of hosts, the whole earth is full of his glory.

On weekdays petitionary prayer follows (the topic in italics is followed by the text of the prayer). The phrase "Praised are you" marks the conclusion of the blessing at hand:

Wisdom–Repentance

You graciously endow man with intelligence;
You teach him knowledge and understanding.
Grant us knowledge, discernment, and wisdom.
Praised are You, O Lord, for the gift of knowledge.

Our Father, bring us back to Your Torah

Our King, draw us near to Your service;
Lead us back to you truly repentant.
Praised are You, O Lord who welcomes repentance.

Forgiveness–Redemption

Our Father, forgive us, for we have sinned;
Our King, pardon us, for we have transgressed;

Enchantment and Transformation: What We Do Together

You forgive sin and pardon transgression.
Praised are You, gracious and forgiving Lord.

Behold our affliction and deliver us

Redeem us soon for the sake of Your name,
For You are the mighty Redeemer.
Praised are You, O Lord, Redeemer of Israel.

Heal Us—Bless Our Years

Heal us, O Lord, and we shall be healed;
Help us and save us, for You are our glory.
Grant perfect healing for all our afflictions,
O faithful and merciful God of healing.
Praised are You, O Lord, Healer of His people.

O Lord our God! Make this a blessed year;
May its varied produce bring us happiness.
Bring blessing upon the whole earth.
Bless the year with Your abounding goodness.
Praised are You, O Lord, who blesses our years.

Gather Our Exiles—Reign Over Us

Sound the great shofar to herald [our] freedom;
Raise high the banner to gather all exiles;
Gather the dispersed from the corners of the earth.
Praised are You, O Lord, who gathers our exiles.

Restore our judges as in days of old;
Restore our counsellors as in former times;

Remove from us sorrow and anguish.
Reign over us alone with lovingkindness;
With justice and mercy sustain our cause.
Praised are You, O Lord, King who loves justice.

Humble the Arrogant—Sustain the Righteous

Frustrate the hopes of those who malign us;
Let all evil very soon disappear;
Let all Your enemies be speedily destroyed.
May You quickly uproot and crush the arrogant;
May You subdue and humble them in our time.
Praised are You, O Lord, who humbles the arrogant.

Let Your tender mercies, O Lord God, be stirred

For the righteous, the pious, the leaders of Israel,
Toward devoted scholars and faithful proselytes.
Be merciful to us of the house of Israel;
Reward all who trust in You;
Cast our lot with those who are faithful to You.
May we never come to despair, for our trust is in You.
Praised are You, O Lord, who sustains the righteous.

Favor Your City and Your People

Have mercy, O Lord, and return to Jerusalem, Your
city;
May Your Presence dwell there as You promised.
Rebuild it now, in our days and for all time;
Re-establish there the majesty of David, Your servant.
Praised are You, O Lord, who rebuilds Jerusalem.

[185]

Bring to flower the shoot of Your servant David

> Hasten the advent of the Messianic redemption;
> Each and every day we hope for Your deliverance.
> Praised are You, O Lord, who assures our deliverance.

O Lord, our God, hear our cry!

> Have compassion upon us and pity us;
> Accept our prayer with loving favor.
> You, O God, listen to entreaty and prayer.
> O King, do not turn us away unanswered,
> For You mercifully heed Your people's supplication.
> Praised are You, O Lord, who is attentive to prayer.

O Lord, Our God, favor Your people Israel

> Accept with love Israel's offering of prayer;
> May our worship be ever acceptable to You.
> May our eyes witness Your return in mercy to Zion.
> Praised are You, O Lord, whose Presence returns to
> Zion.

Our Thankfulness

> We thank You, O Lord our God and God of our
> fathers,
> Defender of our lives, Shield of our safety;
> Through all generations we thank You and praise You.
> Our lives are in Your hands, our souls in Your charge.
> We thank You for the miracles which daily attend us,

For Your wonders and favor morning, noon, and night.
You are beneficent with boundless mercy and love.
From of old we have always placed our hope in You.
For all these blessings, O our King,
We shall ever praise and exalt You.
Every living creature thanks You, and praises You in
truth.
O God, You are our deliverance and our help. Selah!
Praised are You, O Lord, for Your Goodness and Your
glory.

Peace and Well-Being

Grant peace and well-being to the whole house of Israel;
Give us of Your grace, Your love, and Your mercy.
Bless us all, O our Father, with the light of Your
Presence.
It is Your light that revealed to us Your life-giving
Torah,
And taught us love and tenderness, justice, mercy, and
peace.
May it please You to bless Your people in every season,
To bless them at all times with Your fight of peace.
Praised are You, O Lord, who blesses Israel with peace.

The first two petitions pertain to intelligence. Israel thanks
God for mind: knowledge, wisdom, discernment. But knowledge is for a purpose, and the purpose is knowledge of Torah.
Such discernment leads to the service of God and produces a
spirit of repentance. We cannot pray without setting ourselves
right with God, and that means repenting for what has separated us from God. Torah is the way to repentance and to

return. So knowledge leads to Torah, Torah to repentance, and repentance to God. The logical next stop is the prayer for forgiveness. That is the sign of return. God forgives sin; God is gracious and forgiving. Once we discern what we have done wrong through the guidance of Torah, we therefore seek to be forgiven. It is sin that leads to affliction. Affliction stands at the beginning of the way to God; once we have taken that way, we ask for our suffering to end; we beg redemption. This is then specified. We ask for healing, salvation, a blessed year. Healing without prosperity means we may suffer in good health or starve in a robust body. So along with the prayer for healing goes the supplication for worldly comfort.

The individual's task is done. But what of the community? Health and comfort are not enough. The world is unredeemed. Jews are enslaved, in exile, and alien. At the end of days, a great *shofar,* or ram's horn, will sound to herald the Messiah's coming—as is now besought. Israel at prayer asks first for the proclamation of freedom, then for the ingathering of the exiles to the Promised Land. Establishing the messianic kingdom, God needs also to restore a wise and benevolent government, good judges, good counsellors, and loving justice. Meanwhile Israel finds itself maligned. As the prayer sees things, arrogant men hating Israel hate God as well. They should be humbled. And the pious and righteous—the scholars, the faithful proselytes, the whole House of Israel that trusts in God—should be rewarded and sustained. Above all, remember Jerusalem. Rebuild the city and dwell there. Set up Jerusalem's messianic king, David, and make him to prosper. These are the themes of the daily prayer: personal atonement, good health, and good fortunes; collective redemption, freedom, the end of alienation, good government, and true justice; the final and complete salvation of the land and of Jerusalem by the Messiah. At the end comes a prayer that prayer may be heard and found acceptable; then an expression of thanksgiving, not for what may come but for the miracles and mercies already enjoyed morning, noon, and night. And at the end is the prayer for peace—a peace that consists of wholeness for the sacred community.

The third of the three components of the communal worship draws the community outward into the world. When Jews complete any service of worship, they mark its conclusion by making a statement concerning themselves in the world: the corporate community looking outward. Every synagogue service concludes with a prayer prior to going forth, called *Alenu*, from its first word in Hebrew. Like the Exodus, the moment of the congregation's departure becomes a celebration of Israel's God, a self-conscious, articulated rehearsal of Israel's peoplehood. But now it is the end, rather than the beginning, of time that is important. When Jews go forth, they look forward:

Let us praise Him, Lord over all the world;
Let us acclaim Him, Author of all creation.
He made our lot unlike that of other peoples;
He assigned to us a unique destiny.
We bend the knee, worship, and acknowledge
The King of kings, the Holy One, praised is He.
He unrolled the heavens and established the earth;
His throne of glory is in the heavens above;
His majestic Presence is in the loftiest heights.
He and no other is God and faithful King,
Even as we are told in His Torah:
Remember now and always, that the Lord is God;
Remember, no other is Lord of heaven and earth.

We, therefore, hope in You, O Lord our God,
That we shall soon see the triumph of Your might,
That idolatry shall be removed from the earth,
And false gods shall be utterly destroyed.
Then will the world be a true kingdom of God,
When all mankind will invoke Your name,
And all the earth's wicked will return to You.
Then all the inhabitants of the world will surely know
That to You every knee must bend,
Every tongue must pledge loyalty.
Before You, O Lord, let them bow in worship,
Let them give honor to Your glory.
May they all accept the rule of Your kingdom.
May You reign over them soon through all time.
Sovereignty is Yours in glory, now and forever.
So it is written in Your Torah:
The Lord shall reign for ever and ever.

Difference—in secular terms, a people's forming a separate, distinct group—here becomes destiny. Israel thanks God that it enjoys a unique destiny. But the community asks that He who made their lot unlike that of all others will soon rule as sovereign over *all*. The secular difference, which stands for the unique destiny, is for the time being only. When the destiny is fulfilled, there will be no further difference. The natural eye beholds a social group defined by particular cultural characteristics. The myth of peoplehood transforms *difference* into *destiny*.

The premise of obligatory public worship is simple. The existence of the natural group means little, except as testimony to the sovereignty of the God who shaped the group and rules its life. The unique, the particular, the private now are no longer profane matters of culture, but become testimonies of divine sovereignty, pertinent to all people, all groups. The particularism of the group is for the moment alone; the will of God is for eternity. When that will will be done, then all people will recognize that the unique destiny of Israel was intended for everyone. The ordinary facts of sociology no longer predominate. Theology takes over, in the mythic form, the story of eternal truths. The myth of Israel, God's holy people, has changed the secular and commonplace into the paradigm of true being. Public worship requires recitation of words that form worlds, and the words I have reviewed form a complete and cogent statement. But synagogues constituted for public worship succeed only seldom in filling their seats; and, for the most part, daily worship is conducted by a few heroic people; most who participate are obliged to recite the memorial *kaddish* for the deceased. Even daily worship, therefore, so functions as to form an aspect of the life of the family.

Why should this be so? Not because one set of words makes more, or less, sense than another. The words of the prayers hardly appeal to beliefs less reasonable or less grounded in the perceived facts of the real world than the words that transform the rites of passage into re-enactments of mythic being. Quite to the contrary, the creed, the petition, the prayer of departure contain affirmations of Israel as a supernatural entity before God, making a remarkably encompassing statement of the fundamental facts of existence as the faith defines them. As I have already suggested, we cannot appeal solely to the credible contents of one rite to explain its power or to the fantastic allegations of another rite to account for its neglect. Words work when the imagination makes them work; in our minds, we make and therefore remake our world. Those words that in their primary propositions retain powerful appeal address a circumstance that makes them welcome—as fail to do the words that leave us Jews in general untouched and make no difference in shaping our world.

Words enchant in one setting, bore in another, because of the circumstance in which they are recited and the context of life's experience in which they are heard, not because of their propositions. The premise of prayer in the synagogue is simple. Public prayer is something we do together because it is our task. It is our task because we constitute corporate Israel and say our prayers as a community or a social entity. Synagogue prayers then create that social entity, that Israel, just as other prayers at life's passages call into being the world of Eden or, through recalling Egypt and Exodus, express a certain resentment.

The upshot is simple. My prayers speak of an experience I have had. They evoke a world I have known. But what if I know no community beyond myself and immediate family and close friends? Then the words will not evoke a world I can identify. And if that is so, then I also cannot respond to these prayers at all. The problem of prayer is that it is supposed to change the individual and turn that person into part of a community. Prayer, then, is a public action and a statement made by a community. But when there is no sense of community and no experience of a corporate body, then prayers of this kind will refer to a world I have not known, and will not change or even touch the world I have known.

Now this is a generation of home and family, where Jews understand religion as essentially private and personal; and to them supernatural collectivities such as holy Israel, a corporate community before God, have little appeal. Experiences in life that everyone may have—such as hunger and satisfaction, having a baby, feeling different, or getting married—undergo transformation because they refer to facts of life that are very real to us. But to what shared experience does public worship appeal, beyond an obligation to say the prayers? None, if we are to judge by the testimony that the boring, bare, empty synagogues from day to day and Sabbath to Sabbath says. God lives for Israel—but not there. The fault lies not with the synagogue; surely not with the rabbi, who gives his or her life for Judaism; but with this-worldly Israel's social premise. What turns individuals and families into something larger than themselves, changing the *is* into an *as if* of a shared, social metaphor? A provocative question, and one that precipitates a self-evidently valid answer.

The passage through life makes me wonder about love and marriage, birth and family, aging, death. Life in society presents to me questions about who I am in relation to others like me in "being Jewish" or not like me. To answer those questions, I plausibly invoke enchantment, pretending to be something different from, more than what I seem to be. The *is* becomes *as if* when the everyday demands it. Shall I then conclude that no experience shared beyond self and family links Jew to Jew into *an* Israel? Nothing could be more wrong. Jews form a variety of *Israels*—but nothing in their experience today evokes for them that Israel that, within the economy of the sacred, stands before God. The reason is that, for Jews as for others in American and Canadian societies, religion is personal. What forms families into communities are experiences of a different order altogether, which invoke a different set of metaphors from those Jews conceive to be religious. To these other metaphors—those that interpret corporate experience in what are deemed appropriate, therefore essentially political, terms—I now turn.

CHAPTER 12

Two Judaisms: The Dual Torah and Holocaust and Redemption

THE JEWS form a group not merely because they agree on certain propositions on which outsiders do not, but because they exhibit certain public traits that differentiate them from others. The appearance of indifference to the corporate dimensions of the holy life of Judaism should not deceive us. Not only do Jews form a corporate community and share a substantial range of social experience, but that shared social experience in politics also takes form in transformations of the given into a gift, so that the *is* of the everyday polity shades into the *as if* of another time and place, as much as in the transformation by the Judaism of the dual Torah of the passage of the individual through the cycle of life. European, American, and Canadian Jews in politics as much as in private life see themselves in the model of an imagined paradigm, one in substance different from, but in structure the same as, the Passover *seder:* that is, "as if they were liberated." Jews conduct public business, with remarkable unanimity, as though they were somewhere else and someone else than where and what and who they are. Specifically, in politics, in history, in society, even in economics, Jews in North America may not only point to shared traits and experience but also claim to exhibit a viewpoint in common that leads to readily discerned patterns of belief and behavior. Judaism works because of its capacity to turn social fact into fantasy.

The wings of angels beat. We feel the breeze as we pass through life, but not all the time. At home, with family we feel, we hear the voice of silence. Elsewhere, there are other voices. What people do together and share also passes under the transforming power of imagination. What they do not share is not subject to that metamorphosis of vision that changes the *is* into the *as if*. Everything that, in the religious life of Judaism, works its wonder for the generality of Jews proves personal and familial, not communal—and does so despite the remarkable fact of Jewish distinctiveness within the larger society of America and, all the more so, Canada. The social experience forms the premise of the religious life. But the Jews' social experience of polity and community does not match the religious experience of home and family. Hence the religious side to things conforms to the boundaries of family; and the public experience of politics, economics, and society that Jews share comes to expression in different ways altogether. I see two fundamental reasons for the present state of affairs, which finds the religion, Judaism, intensely affective in the private life and remarkably irrelevant to the public. The one reason is the prevailing attitude toward religion and its correct realm; the other is the Jews' reading of their experience of the twentieth century, which has defined as the paramount mode of interpreting social experience a paradigm other than that deriving from the life of that Israel that is the holy people of mind and imagination, therefore also of sanctification and salvation. Let me explain what I mean by the first of the two, the definition of the proper place of religion in public and political life.

Two Judaisms—the one of the dual Torah, the other of Holocaust and Redemption—flourish side by side, the one viewed as self-evidently valid at home, the other taken to be obvious and beyond all need of proof or demonstration in the public discourse. The words that in the Jews' life as a group evoke worlds that transform, that reach public and socially shared emotions to turn occasions into events, speak—just as does the liturgy of the synagogue—of murder and survival. The topic now is public policy, politics, how we should relate to the world beyond. And, in the nature of public life in North America, that topic is taken to be not otherworldly and super- natural (Adam and Eve in Eden indeed!), but this-worldly and political, involving the affairs of nations and states. The re- ceived Judaism of the dual Torah—with its Adam and Eve, Abraham, Isaac, and Jacob, slaves in Egypt, Moses on Sinai, sanctification in the here and now and salvation at the end of time—that Judaism exercises power at home. But it is not understood to, and does not, pertain to the issues of public policy and politics that Jewry as a collectivity chooses to address. That other Judaism, which speaks of history and poli- tics, things that have really happened and their implications in the here and now, takes over when the Jew leaves home.

If, as we have seen, the received Judaism thrives in the private life of home and family, where, in general, religion in North America is understood to work its wonders, that other Judaism makes its way in the public arena, where, in general, function politics and public policy, viewed as distinct from religion. That other Judaism—the one of Holocaust and Re- demption rather than Eden, Sinai, and the World to Come—

is, we recognize, political in its themes and character, myth and rites. The world view of the Judaism of Holocaust and Redemption evokes political, historical events—the destruction of the Jews in Europe, the creation of the State of Israel, two events of a wholly political character. It treats these events as unique, just as the Judaism of the dual Torah treats as unique Eden and Adam's fall, Sinai, and the coming redemption. The Judaism of the Holocaust and Redemption, finding in these events the ultimate meaning of the life of the Jews together as Israel, therefore defines an Israel for itself—the State of Israel in particular—just as the Judaism of the dual Torah finds in Eden, Sinai, and the world to come the meaning of the life of Israel and so defines for itself an Israel too: the holy Israel, the social entity different in its very essence from all other social entities. That other Judaism, the Judaism of Holocaust and Redemption, addresses the issues of politics and public policy that Jews take up in their collective social activity.

When we ask why the bifurcation between the personal and the familial, subjected to the Judaism of the dual Torah, perceived as religion; and the public and civic, governed by the Judaism of Holocaust and Redemption, perceived as politics—we turn outward. For the explanation lies in the definition of permissible difference in North America and the place of religion in that difference. Specifically, in North American society, defined as it is by Protestant conceptions, it is permissible to be different in religion, *but* religion is a matter of what is personal and private. Hence, Judaism as a religion encompasses what is personal and familial. The Jews as a political entity, then, put forth a separate system, one that concerns not religion, which is not supposed to intervene in political action, but public policy. Judaism in public policy produces political action in favor of the State of Israel, or Soviet Jewry, or other important matters of the corporate community. Judaism in private affects the individual and the family and is not supposed to play a role in politics at all. That pattern conforms to the Protestant model of religion, and the Jews have accomplished conformity to it by means of making up two Judaisms. A consideration of the Protestant pattern, which separates not the institutions of Church from the activities of the state, but the entire public polity from the inner life, will show us how to make sense of the presence of the two Judaisms of North America.

Here in Protestant North America, as I have said, people commonly see religion as something personal and private: prayer, for example, speaks for the individual. No wonder, then, that those enchanted words and gestures that Jews adopt transform the inner life, recognize life's transitions and turn them into rites of passage. It is part of a larger prejudice that religion and rite speak to the heart of the particular person. What can be changed by rite, then, is first of all personal and private, not social, not an issue of culture, not affective in politics, not part of the public interest. What people do when they respond to religion, therefore, affects an interior world—a world with little bearing on the realities of public discourse: what, in general terms, we should do about nuclear weapons; or, in terms of Judaism, how we should organize and imagine society. The transformations of religion do involve not the world, or even the self as representative of other selves, but mainly the individual at the most unique and unrepresentative. If God speaks to me in particular, then the message, by definition, is mine—not someone else's. Religion, the totality of these private messages (within the present theory), therefore does not make itself available for communication in public discourse, and that by definition, too. Religion plays no public role. It is a matter not of public activity but of what people happen to believe or do in private: a matter mainly of the heart.

But the public life of Jewry, reaching religious statement in Judaism, is not trivial, not private, not individual, not a matter only of the heart. Religion is public, political, social, economic. Religion as a powerful force in shaping politics and culture, economic action, and social organization finds its counterpart, within Jewry, as we shall see, in the power of the community of the Jews to generate a Judaism.

Nothing humanity has made constitutes a less personal, a less private, a less trivial fact of human life than religion. Religion, however, is understood in Protestant North America as being individual and subjective: how I feel all by myself, not what I do with other people. The prevailing attitude of mind identifies religion with belief, to the near exclusion of behavior. Religion is understood as a personal state of mind or an individual's personal and private attitude. When we study religion, the present picture suggests, we ask not about society but about self, not about culture and community but about conscience and character. Religion speaks of individuals and not of groups: of faith and its substance, and, beyond faith, of the things that faith represents: faith reified; hence, religion. William Scott Green, professor of religion at the University of Rochester, further comments in more general terms:

The basic attitude of mind characteristic of the study of religion holds that religion is certainly in your soul, likely in your heart, perhaps in your mind, but never in your body. That attitude encourages us to construe religion cerebrally and individually, to think in terms of beliefs and the believer, rather than in terms of behavior and community. The lens provided by this prejudice draws our attention to the intense and obsessive belief called "faith," so religion is understood as a state of mind, the object of intellectual or emotional commitment, the result of decisions to believe or to have faith. According to this model, people have religion but they do not do their religion. Thus we tend to devalue behavior and performance, to make it epiphenomenal and of course to emphasize thinking and reflecting, the practice of theology, as a primary activity of religious people. . . . The famous slogan that "ritual recapitulates myth" follows this model by assigning priority to the story and to peoples' believing the story, and makes behavior simply an imitation, an aping, a mere acting out.*

Now, as we reflect on Green's observations, we recognize what is at stake: it is the definition of religion—or, rather, what matters in or about religion—emerging from Protestant theology and Protestant religious experience.

For when we lay heavy emphasis on faith to the exclusion of works, on the individual rather than on society, on conscience instead of culture; when we treat behavior and performance by groups as less important and thinking, reflecting, theology, and belief as more important—we are adopting as normative for academic scholarship convictions critical to the Protestant Reformation. Judaism and the historical, classical forms of Christianity, Roman Catholic and Orthodox, place emphasis at least equally on religion as a matter of works and not of faith alone, on behavior and community as well as belief and conscience. Religion is something that people do, and they do it together. Religion is not something people merely *have*, as individuals. Since the entire civilization of the West, from

*Personal letter, 17 January 1985.

the fourth century on, carried forward the convictions of Christianity, not about the individual alone but about politics and culture, we may hardly find surprising the Roman Catholic conviction that religion flourishes not alone in heart and mind but in eternal social forms: the Church; in former times, the state as well.

A community of interest and experience such as the Jews comprise will self-evidently appeal to shared values that give expression to common experience, explaining in a single way how diverse individuals and families find it possible to see things in so cogent a manner: this way, not that. The issue, therefore, is not whether a Judaism forms the center, but *which* Judaism. What is important in understanding where and how Judaism is a religion, and where it is not, is this: the two Judaisms coexist, the one in private, the other in public. The Judaism of the dual Torah forms the counterpart to religion in the Protestant model, affecting home and family and private life. The Judaism of Holocaust and Redemption presents the counterpart to religion in the civil framework, making an impact upon public life and policy within the distinctive Jewish community of North America. The relationships between the two Judaisms prove parlous and uneven, since the Judaism of home and family takes second place in public life of Jewry—and public life is where the action takes place in that community.

Not only so, but the Judaism of the dual Torah makes powerful demands on the devotee, for example requiring him or her to frame emotions within a received model of attitudes and appropriate feelings. The Judaism of Holocaust and Redemption, by contrast, provides ready access to emotional or political encounters, easily available to all—by definition. The immediately accessible experiences of politics predominate.

The repertoire of human experience in the Judaism of the dual Torah presents, by contrast, as human options the opposite of the immediate. In this Judaism, Jews receive and use the heritage of human experience captured, as in amber, in the words of the dual Torah. Thus, in public life, Jews focus their imaginative energies upon the Holocaust and their eschatological fantasies on the "beginning of our redemption" in the State of Israel. Two competing Judaisms—the one that works at home, the other in public—therefore coexist on an unequal basis, because the one appeals to easily imagined experience, the other to the power of will to translate and transform the here and the now into something other.

The Judaism of Holocaust and Redemption speaks of exclusion and bigotry, hatred and contempt, and asks us, therefore, to imagine ourselves in gas chambers. All of us have known (though many suppress the knowledge) exclusion. No Jew can imagine himself or herself to be utterly like "everyone else," because the beginning of being a Jew is, by definition, to be different because one is a Jew—whatever the difference may mean. Accordingly, the Judaism of Holocaust and Redemption addresses an experience that is common and—by definition—accessible to all Jews. The Judaism of the dual Torah speaks of God and humanity in God's likeness, after God's image. It calls up the experience of exile and redemption, appealing to corners of experience that, for us as we are, prove empty. The Judaism of the dual Torah demands sensibility, intellect, understanding; it asks us to build bridges from who we are to what the Torah tells us we may become. Not everyone musters the inner energy to imagine, and many do not. No wonder, then, that the Judaism of Holocaust and Redemption enjoys priority over the Judaism of the dual Torah—except in those corners of life, in those private moments of intense personal experience, at which the Torah, and only the Torah, serves to tell us what is happening to us. The competition, as I said, is unequal, because the one Judaism reaches into that sore surface of Jewish life—that is, being different by reason of being Jewish; while the other plumbs the depths of our being human in God's image: not the same thing at all.

And yet—

And yet—if I may make my judgment explicit—the Judaism of the Holocaust and Redemption, with its focus upon the "out there" of public policy and its present pre-eminence, offers as a world nightmares made of words. Its choice of formative experiences, its repertoire of worthwhile human events: these impose upon Jews two devilish enchantments. First, the message of Holocaust and Redemption is that difference is not destiny but disaster—if one trusts the gentiles. Second, the expressions of Holocaust and Redemption—political action, letters to public figures, pilgrimages to grisly places—leave the inner life untouched but distorted. Being Jewish in that Judaism generates fear and distrust of the other, but does not compensate by an appeal to worth and dignity for the self. The Judaism of Holocaust and Redemption leaves the life of individual and family untouched and unchanged. But people live at home and in family. Consequently, the Judaism of Holocaust and Redemption, in ignoring the private life, makes trivial the differences that separate Jew from gentile. People may live a private life of utter neutrality, untouched by the demands of the faith, while working out a public life of acute segregation. The Judaism of Holocaust and Redemption turns on its head the wise policy of the reformers and enlightened of the early nineteenth century: a Jew at home, a citizen "out there." Now it is an undifferentiated American at home, a Jew in the public polity.

[203]

The Judaism of the dual Torah, for its part, proves equally insufficient. Its address to the self and family to the near exclusion of the world beyond leaves awry its fundamental mythic structure, which appeals to history and the end of time, to sanctification and the worth of difference. Viewed whole, each of its components at the passage of life and the passing of one's own life—the disposition of birth, marriage, aging, for example; the encounter with difference—makes sense only in that larger context of public policy. Separating the private and familial from the public and communal distorts the Judaism of the dual Torah. Ignoring the individual and the deeply felt reality of the home leaves the Judaism of Holocaust and Redemption strangely vacant: in the end, a babble of tear-producing, but unfelt, words; a manipulation of emotions for a transient moment. The Judaism of the Holocaust and Redemption is romantic. The Judaism of the dual Torah accomplishes the permanent wedding of Israel, the Jewish people, to God. The one is for hotels; the other, for the home. But both Judaisms speak to our heart—the divided heart today.

That is why we must learn to see the *as if* in the *is,* as did the sages who read Scripture and heard a message about the politics of their age. Since the arts transform life into metaphor and through the power of will and the force of imagination change *is* into *might be,* the very public experience of "being Jewish" in sentiment and sensibility emerges from the mind moving upward when mere words fail: movement beyond message made up of mere words. The message emerges from the moment of pure and holy recognition: yes, that is what it is all about, that is what it means. In that shared perception prior to words and beyond them, creation begins for the world that awaits.

Enchantment beyond Words

WE THINK we are singular. But the world rarely imposes upon us that perception that transforms difference into destiny. We see ourselves as a group, a community. But what makes us a group is not shared experience, of which there is none. What marks us off, in our minds, is that which is different as we think it different from the experience of others and, also, that which is in our imagination also endowed with a special significance. The world tells us the opposite of our distinctiveness: we are like everyone, and everyone is like us. Difference is trivial or deplorable. Sameness, homogeneity—these are the appeals of the commonalities of culture.

But—and this by definition—we feel in our hearts that we are different, we hope with all our minds that we share a common destiny of worth, we aspire in our souls to form a community. And these feelings, hopes, aspirations—this sense of corporate self of Jewry as Israel, children of Abraham and Sarah, Isaac and Rebecca, Jacob and Leah and Rachel—these inner visions flow upward and outward from within the mind's eye and the heart's deepest impulses. That is why, I argue, we live out of imagination. To that inner vision, shared among us all, everything else is commentary. Our text is within.

What can draw us together and persuade us in public, not

only in private, to do one thing and not another and move us and shape our hearts—and also our minds? When we locate the appropriate medium for enchantment, the message for that medium will dictate itself. That medium must now move beyond mere words, and the enchantment must change the heart in the haven where the heart yet shelters: the life beyond words, without words alone or mainly. I speak of the world beyond mere words: the world of poetry, not mere prose; of drama and theater made up of the materials of the everyday; of sound become music and silence; of motion made into movement and mime; of the moving image that captures what is beyond the common sight and vision. This world of art and the arts awaits to do its wonder. If we wish to touch and change people, we turn to the arts, for that is how, as human beings—from the beginning of recorded art, before recorded time—we have said the things that, beyond words, we mean to express. The words that make worlds are artfully formed. Enchantment is a craft, an art, and not a mode of manipulation. In proposing, therefore, to explain how we may transform ourselves after God's command ("in our image, after our likeness"), I appeal to the diverse modes and media of human transformation: the inner eye, the ear that perceives the thin voice of silence, the imagination inside that changes the world "out there." Words change worlds—the right words; moreover, not all signs and wonders come to us in words. The well-crafted sentence, the well-played note, the well-directed scene on stage—these capture our imagination and change it, and we are changed, enchanted.

When words work wonders now, it is because they appeal to us despite ourselves. Moved by life's passages, we listen when liturgy speaks. Touched by the passage of time, we turn to the synagogue and its rites. Experiencing difference, we ask how it may be destiny—and invoke "Holocaust and Redemption." These are the gifts of a world "out there." Our community, in its active role through agencies of religion, education, politics, makes use of our experience, but neither shapes nor enriches it, because the community at large has yet to grasp the power of imagination and the things that nourish it.

Today's Jewish community conducts business principally through propaganda, understood as the medium of the printed word in prose, as though little has changed in the art of communication since the invention of printing. Though the Jews helped create the art of the moving image, the cinema, Jews transmit their traditions without teaching their children to express "being Jewish" with that image, videocamera in hand for instance. Jews in advertising understand the power of the unarticulated symbol, but Jews in the synagogue persist in word mumbling and word mongering as the sole form of worship. Jews stand in the forefront of the international world of all the arts in America and Europe, but Jewry as a matter of public policy has yet to recognize the profoundly artistic gifts within its people, on the one side, and their deep response to the arts, on the other.

Yet in the coming century we will speak as much through symbol and image, gesture and mime, as our ancestors spoke through the Word translated mainly into words. Through the arts, appealing to the heart and soul when words fail, one can speak through song and poetry, voice and silence, hand and foot, paint and stone, film and laser beam. The arts can take a stone and make a sculpture that will move us like a prayer; the artist can take our stony heart and open it to the depths. In my view, the future of a single Judaism, at one with itself in public and in private, will begin when media beyond the prose of words alone so take shape as to impart to Jewry, that distinct and distinctive community, a Judaism of experience encompassing both the message of the dual Torah and the anguished memory, so near at hand and painful, of our sorrow and our joy in Europe and in the State of Israel. Through art, Jews will move from worlds made out of words to worlds transformed in imagination and the educated inner eye.

We are Jews through the power of our imagination. To be a Jew is at its foundations an act of art. It is to perceive the ordinary as simile and the received as metaphor. It is through will and heart and soul to turn what we are into something more than we imagine we can be. The Jews' task is to make ourselves, souls, lives, into works of art. This surpassing act of art we do through art: poetry, drama, music, dance, the arts of the eye and the arts of the soul and the arts of the folk alike. Setting the Sabbath table is an act of art. Carrying the Torah in the synagogue processional is an act of dance. Composing a prayer and reciting a prayer are acts of poetry and drama. The memorial and commemoration of the murder of six million Jews in Europe take the form of film and fiction even now. All of these point the way in which we must go.

It is the arts' enchantment of Jewish existence, worked through poetry not prose, through music not uncadenced speech, that transforms one thing into something else. For our human existence as Jews requires us to turn one place, in the here and now, into another place, in time to come or times past and always, a thing into a different thing: humanity into God's image and after God's likeness, the ultimate transformation of creation. Time becomes a different time; space, a different place; gesture and mime, more than what they seem; assembled people, a social entity, a being that transcends the human beings gathered together: a nation, a people, a community. Scripture, prayers, formulas of faith—these form mere words, define categories other than those contributed by the here and now.

To be a Jew is to live both *as if* and also in the here and now. By *as if* I mean that we form in our minds and imaginations a picture of ourselves that the world we see every day does not sustain. We are more than we seem, other than we appear to be. To be a Jew is to live a metaphor, to explore the meaning of life as simile, of language as poetry and of action as drama and of vision as art. For Scripture begins with the judgment of humanity that we are "in our image, after our likeness"; and once humanity forms image and likeness, we are not what we seem but something different, something more. And for Israel, the Jewish people, the metaphor takes over in the comparison and contrast between what we appear to be and what in the image, after the likeness of the Torah, we are told we really are.

That task of sculpting life into art, and imagining life as it must be, begins not in politics but in theology, when in Scripture we read: "Let us make Adam in our image, after our likeness." To see a human being and to perceive God—that is what it means to be a Jew, so Scripture says. And that is an act of art, a moment of artistic truth, to be carried out alone by poetry, not by prose; alone by theater, not by ordinary speech; alone by dance, not by clumsy and ordinary shuffling; alone by the silence of disciplined sound we know as music, not by background noise and rackets; alone by the eye of the artist who sees within and beyond, not by the vacant stare of those who do not even see what is there.

Words refer to revelation, appeal to God; they do not merely make explicit but affirm attitude and feeling and trust. Standing for acceptance and submission, response and renewal and regeneration, words, in the end, in Judaism are therefore not the thing, the religion, but merely the name of the thing: the notes, as I said, that tell us how to make the religion. Upon time, space, deed, assembly, Judaism works its wonder through word and gesture, song and speech, denoting persons, things, God—throughout, in art. Definite objective rules, set sequences of words and acts, work the wonder of enchantment, turning water into wine, turning the family assembled for a meal into slaves escaping from Egypt, and common folk into Israel, God's people, each in its proper time and place. And it is how, too, we endure the six million murders, one by one, that torment us every day. That, too, can form an act of the imagination, nourished by the right words, said in the right way.

I do not speak of mere mumbled incantation. Far from it. The words convey propositions, and rites stand for truths that we can express. But Judaic existence is not in the words, the emotions, the attitudes alone. Judaism takes place through art, in enchantment that transforms, changing something into something else, somewhere into anywhere, some time into all time. And therefore we can say not that Judaism *is,* but rather that Judaism *takes place* at that moment at which in our imagination, expressed through the media of heart and intellect beyond all speech, we enter into the circle of the sacred and through words of enchantment transform the world, if only for a moment. That is where God takes place.

We turn to art, specifically, to solve a concrete problem that we Jewish Americans confront. It is the lack of a world beyond to which we may refer as we refer to the murder of our people in Europe from 1933 to 1945: that is, we refer to the experiences of others in framing our Judaic world but do not have immediate access, except in the rites of passage and the intensely personal moments of renewal, to experiences of our own that generate and frame a world beyond. I can best describe this void by contrasting our lives to the Israelis' lives as Jews. To be a Jew in the State of Israel is to live—so Israelis tell us—a Jewish life that is whole, complete, concrete and material and everyday. They live in a Jewish land. We do not. They live by the Jewish calendar. We do not. They speak the very particular Jewish language, Hebrew. We speak the nearly universal language, English. In these and many other ways, they are the players, we are the fans. Israelis live out their Jewish identity in the air they breathe, the sights they see, the language of their being. We kiss through a veil and read about love, so to speak.

But through art, we can gain access to that same experience of a direct and unmediated encounter: in expressing our sensibility and feeling through all the media that convey art, we do not talk *about* Jewish things, we talk Jewish words. We do not hear and applaud, we make the music. We are the actors on a stage of our own invention. The arts form that unmediated medium for the living out of our Jewish identity. For through the arts, we enlist our imagination in that act of creation that forms and frames our Jewish existence. Direct and unmediated, the arts touch us, because we can touch ourselves, feel for ourselves, respond within ourselves. So the experience of the arts may form that homeland within, that private sphere we share with others like ourselves, that life being Jewish promises us. Lived out in heart and soul and mind, in North and Latin America and Canada, Europe, Africa, the far Pacific, we may indeed undertake a direct encounter with our Jewish being by reason of the power of creative arts. Israelis contend that they are Jews by reason of their politics. But the greatest act of the Jewish imagination of this century (and as a Zionist, I think, many other centuries past) is the creation of the State of Israel—which took place first in heart and mind and only then in the concrete and material world of politics. *All of us are Jews through the power of our imagination.*

That is how, in the age in which we live, it should be. But that is not *how* it is. For we Jews, who number among us great poets and writers, great actors and directors and playwrights and producers, great musicians and composers, we Jews who fill the theaters and concert halls and museums and galleries, we Jews in our community life pretend the arts have nothing to give us, and we nothing to do with them. We are conscious only that we live in the here and now, but our life together points toward eternity past and future. We pretend that we talk prose but our common life together speaks in poetry. In the age of mass communication, television and video and powerful visual stimuli, in the era of music everywhere, in the moment at which poetry, transforming words into power, takes the place of prose—for all advertising copy is an exercise in poetry—and at which the moving image of film and television shapes our vision and our intellect, the Jewish community remains tied to the written word, said as lifeless prose: propaganda. We use words without art, ignoring poetry, liturgy, and text. We pretend that we express ourselves mainly in writing masses of unfelt words, and that people shape their perceptions mainly in reading without responding. That is the pretense that we Jews maintain because we think we are smart and intellectual. Our intellectual tradition itself is a work of surpassing art. But so far as it is mere prose, it requires the balance of the arts and the stimulus of the arts. The museum, the stage, and the concert hall—these, too, form the realm of intellect and expression. The arts, specifically, comprise those other media of human expression, and the arts affect those other modes of communication that, everywhere but in the heart of the Jewish community, draw people together and persuade them to do one thing and not another and move them and shape their hearts—and also their minds.

Now if it were the case that, whatever the arts can do for us, we Jews are not a people of the arts, then I could understand today's neglect within the organized Jewish community of the promise and prospects of the arts in all their disciplines. In fact, however, we Jews number among us artists of every discipline too numerous to count. No field of the arts—whether in the written or the spoken word, whether in sound or sight, whether in movement or mime, whether on the stage or the street—but has its Jewish stars, and no firmament of the arts in America could survive, and still shine so brilliantly, the loss of its Jewish stars.

Well, one might say, those Jewish geniuses of the arts are one thing, but the community at large does not respond anyhow. Yet take away the Jews and where are the museums and the symphony orchestras and the theaters? Gone are the audiences, gone the patrons, gone the galleries and their customers—not all, but a significant proportion of them. So here we have the paradox: the arts thrive because of Jewish artists and Jewish audiences, and entire fields of American artistic achievement have come to fruition because of gifted Jews. And yet the Jewish community has yet to learn that the arts are here to help us be who we are, to make the statement that is ours. We are pretending that we are other than what we really are: people who either sing and dance, turn speech into drama, tell stories, mime, sculpt, paint, draw, speak through the moving image—or respond to those who do.

For me, it follows, a Jewish community that affirms its future will require not only a synagogue rich in drama and choreography, but also a museum actively engaged in educating the community at large; also a theater constantly compelling people to pretend and to imagine and to respond; also an orchestra drawing upon the resources of music to create, in the magic moment of performance, a mode of Jewish existence. Just as every community today understands that it must have rabbis and cantors, teachers and social workers, executives of federations and managers of institutions, so every community tomorrow will have to look for its poets, its playwrights and actors, its graphic artists, its dancers and choreographers, and directors and design artists and folk artists and singers and conductors and composers: the Jews who, rich in imagination, can teach us by example how to imagine ourselves as Jews, just as rabbis or teachers teach by example. *We are Jews through the power of our imagination.*

Through the arts, Jews have given to America and the West a universally accessible message. Just as there is no field of artistic expression in which Jews have not excelled, so is there none in which they have not made a statement of universal meaning. Indeed, it was through their prominence in the arts that Jews first attained a normal status in this country and the West in general: as people whom others could understand and with whom they could engage. Through the arts, we have made ourselves less strange and more normal, into Americans or British or French—but of a particular sort. Now, I am inclined to think that we make contradictory demands upon America and upon ourselves. We wish to be undifferentiated and ordinary, when we choose to be; and to be highly differentiated and extraordinary, when we choose to be; and to decide between the two, also whenever we choose. We want to be treated like everyone else, and we are right. We want to be special, and we are right. And we want to decide. And we are right—and, in making these contradictory demands, we are like everyone else.

What can resolve the ineluctable tension between difference and sameness, between being "ourselves"—in Judaic terms, individuals within home and family—but also part of the group—in Judaic terms, part of the civil religion of the Judaic polity? What can make us one, whole and integrated, different and alike, particular and universal, at once and the same time, is this: the singular moment when, through being our most individual, we also speak to an experience that is most general. And what can capture and convey that particular moment constitutes our claim upon the community beyond, for the medium that speaks to the other concerning the self bears the message that the *I* can speak to the other who is a *thou,* a *you.* Now to me it is obvious that the artist, on the long voyage within, brings back messages to us outside—that is, to the other "out there." On a journey into the imagination, the dancer, absorbed in physical gesture and movements of grace, concentrates on the dance. But we, the other, respond to the vision. On a trip beyond, the writer and the poet seek individual language for a private moment—the language that is meant not only to express but also to convey. And so with music, and so with art, and so with drama whether on the stage or in film, and so with glass and tapestry and graphics. When we are most ourselves, we are most at one with the other. From deep "in here" we speak to the vast spaces "out there." When, within the arts, we delve deep within what is private and personal and particular and Jewish, we discover that humanity within that stands for, and therefore both speaks to and evokes, humanity "out there."

To be a Jew is to engage in an act of creation, which is to

be like God in the vision of the serpent. When the serpent argues with Woman and Man to take of the fruit of the tree of knowledge of good and evil, the serpent tells them that God knows that, when they eat of the fruit of that tree, they will become like God. On this, Rashi, the great Jewish interpreter of Scripture, has commented, "Creators of worlds." We have eaten of the fruit. We are creators of worlds. For good or ill, we live by our power to create, beginning with the strength of intellect and imagination to create ourselves: something out of nothing—before, in death, we return to nothing, and wait.

NOTES

Bibliographical Note

This theology of Judaism out of the liturgical life of the faith focuses upon the Siddur, or Jewish Prayerbook, and counterpart materials for the festivals and holy days. A full bibliography and discussion of some of the problems of liturgy is in Richard S. Sarason, "Siddur," in Jacob Neusner, ed., *The Study of Ancient Judaism* (New York: Ktav, 1981), vol. I, *Mishnah, Midrash, Siddur*, pp. 92–188.

In addition, an authoritative account of the history and formation of the liturgy of Judaism is provided by Lawrence A. Hoffman, *The Canonization of the Synagogue Service* (Notre Dame: University of Notre Dame Press, 1979). Hoffman covers every item treated here—the Passover *Haggadah*, the *Shema*, the Prayer (Eighteen Benedictions) and the *kaddish*, the festival and holiday liturgy, the prayers of the life cycle and Grace after Meals—and also provides a thorough account of the process by which the liturgy achieved canonical status. The sizable scholarly literature down to 1979 is reviewed in his notes. Sarason's bibliography and Hoffman's major scholarly work together provide a definitive picture of the history and development of the liturgy of Judaism.

Preface

1. Abraham Joshua Heschel, *The Sabbath: Its Meaning for Modern Man* (New York: Farrar, Straus, 1948).

2. Jacob Neusner, *Self-Fullfilling Prophecy: Exile and Return in the History of Judaism* (Boston: Beacon Press, 1987); Jacob Neusner, *Death and Birth of Judaism: The Impact of Christianity, Secularism, and the Holocaust on Jewish Faith* (New York: Basic Books, 1987).

Chapter 1. The World Out There: Contemporary Judaism

1. I have been guided throughout by Israel Scheffler's *Inquiries: Philosophical Studies of Language, Science and Learning* (Indianapolis: Hackett Publishing, 1986), pp. 41–80; epigraph to this chapter from p. 67.

Notes

2. Calvin Goldscheider, *Jewish Continuity and Change: Emerging Patterns in America* (Bloomington: Indiana University Press, 1986), pp. 170, 171.

Chapter 3. The Rite of Circumcision: The "Others" Who Come to Celebrate

1. Lifsa Schachter, "Reflections on the Brit Mila Ceremony," *Conservative Judaism* 38 (1986):38–41.
2. *Pirke deRabbi Eliezer,* trans. Gerald Friedlander (London, 1916), pp. 212–14.
3. Schachter, "Reflections," p. 41.

Chapter 4. The Marriage Ceremony: *You* and *I* Become Adam and Eve

1. Jules Harlow, ed., *A Rabbi's Manual* (New York: Rabbinical Assembly, 1965), p. 32.

Chapter 6. Sabbaths of Creation, Festivals of Redemption: Turning from the World to Rest

1. Abraham Joshua Heschel, *The Sabbath: Its Meaning for Modern Man* (New York: Farrar, Straus, 1948), pp. 216–17.
2. Heschel cited in Fritz A. Rothschild, ed., *Between God and Man: An Interpretation of Judaism: From the Writings of Abraham J. Heschel* (New York: Harper, 1959), p. 222.
3. Ibid., pp. 226–27.
4. Ibid., p. 229.
5. Ibid., p. 215.
6. Ibid., p. 218.

Chapter 8. Jewish Law and Learning: The *Halakhah* and *Talmud Torah*

1. Babylonian Talmud tractate Shabbat, p. 31(a).
2. Ibid.

Notes

3. Babylonian Talmud tractate Makkot, p. 24(a).
4. Leviticus Rabbah XIII:V.9.
5. Ibid., V.10.
6. Ibid., V.12.
7. Ibid., V.13.

Chapter 9. The *Bar* (with and without) *Mitzvah*

1. Jacob Neusner, *Death and Birth of Judaism: The Impact of Christianity, Secularism, and the Holocaust on Jewish Faith* (New York: Basic Books, 1987), pp. 324–31.

Chapter 10. Death: The Silent World of Real Dirt and Ashes

1. Jules Harlow, ed., *A Rabbi's Manual* (New York: Rabbinical Assembly, 1965), p. 130.
2. Mishnah tractate Sanhedrin 11:1.
3. Babylonian Talmud tractate Sanhedrin 90A-B, section I.
4. Ibid., section II.
5. Ibid., section IV.
6. Ibid., section V.
7. Ibid., section VI.
8. Ibid., section VII.
9. Ibid., section VIII–IX.
10. Ibid., section XII.
11. Ibid., section XIII.

GENERAL INDEX

Abayye, 160

Alenu, 10, 22, 174

Ammi, 162

Aqiba, 131, 160–61

Assimilation, contemporary Judaism and world view, 13–28

Birth, circumcision rite, 43–52

Blessings: in circumcision rite, 43–52; Seven Blessings, marriage ceremony, 57–60; *see also* Grace after Meals

Christianity, and conceptions of Judaism, 197–200

Circumcision, 98, 108, 115; and covenant of Abraham, 43–52; in liturgical life of Judaism, 9

Cohen, Boaz, 147

Commandments: *bar* and *bat mitzvah,* 139–145; eleventh, 23; reduction of original, of Moses, 121–23

Community life, 7–9; and *bar* and *bat mitzvah,* 139–45; contemporary Judaism and world view of, 13–28; and Jewish law and study of Torah, 114–36; in life of Judaism, 7–9; and synagogue life, 167–93

Confession at onset of death, 147–48

Contemporary Judaism: assimilation and world view of, 13–28; Dual Torah and world view of, 17–19, 21–28; and world view of home and family, 19–28

Day of Atonement (Yom Kippur), 100–13; in liturgical life of Judaism, 9–10, 12, 15;

and Passover *seder,* freedom from bondage, 69–84

Days of Awe, 10, 85, 87, 100–13, 115

Deeds and gestures, enchantment of religion, 7

Dual Torah in Judaism, 194–204; and communal life, 167–93; contemporary Judaism and world view of, 17–19, 21–28

Eighteen Benedictions, 10, 170, 174, 181–88

Eliezer b. R. Yose, 160

Elisha, curse of, 155

Exodus, Passover *seder,* freedom from bondage, 69–84

Fackenheim, Emil, 23

Family, *see* Home and family

Feast of Weeks *(Shavuot),* 96–98, 107

Festival of Tabernacles, *see* Sukkot

Festivals, 115; Psalms for Sabbaths and, 33–34; of redemption, 85–99; *see also* Sabbaths and festivals

Gamaliel, 157–58

Goldscheider, Calvin, 19–20

Government and politics, *see* Community life

Grace after Meals, 9, 31–42, 98, 115

Green, William Scott, 199

Halakhah, see Jewish law

Heschel, Abraham Joshua, 85, 89–91, 94–95

Hillel, 121

General Index

Hilqiah, 130

Holocaust and Redemption, Judaism of, 21–22, 24–26, 194–204

Home and family: contemporary Judaism and world view of, 19–28; as holy place, 7–9; Jewish law and study of Torah in, 114–36; and marriage ceremony, Adam and Eve, 53–65; and Passover *seder*, 69–84; ritual purity of meals in, 34–37

Huppah, see Marriage ceremony

Ishmael, 160–61

Israel, State of, *see* State of Israel

Jewish law *(Halakhah)*, 114–36; death and burial rites in, 146–63

Jewish Theological Seminary of America, 5

Jonathan, 155

Joshua b. Hananiah, 159

Judah, 155

Judah b. R. Simon, 129

Judaism: Christian conceptions of, 197–200; community life and, 7–9; contemporary, and world view, 13–28; dual Torah in, 17–19, 21–28, 194–204; of Holocaust and Redemption, 21–22, 24–26, 194–204; *see also* Liturgy in life of Judaism

Kaddish (memorial prayer), 108, 149–51, 191

Ketubah (marriage contract), 58

Kol Nidre, see Vows

Liturgy in life of Judaism: and *Alenu*, 10, 22, 174; and circumcision, 9; contemporary Judaism and world view of, 17, 21; and Day of Atonement, 9–10, 12, 15; and Days of Awe, 10, 100–13; Eighteen Benedictions in, 10, 170, 174, 181–88; and festivals of redemption, 85–99; and Grace after Meals, 9, 31–42, 98, 115; and marriage ceremony, 9; New Year prayers in, 9, 100–13; and Rosh Hashanah, 9, 100–13; Sabbaths of creation in, 85–99; and *Shema*, 10, 40, 169–70, 172, 174–81; and synagogue life, 167–93; and Yom Kippur, 9–10, 12, 15; *see also* Passover *seder*, Sabbaths and festivals

Marriage ceremony, 98, 108; individuals of, as Adam and Eve, 53–65; in liturgical life of Judaism, 9

Maturity, and *bar* and *bat mitzvah*, 139–45

Messianic hope, 108; in burial rites, 149–50; in Grace after Meals, 26–37, 41

Neusner, Eli, 45–46

New Year, Days of Awe, 9, 100–13

Pappa, 160

Passover *seder*, freedom from bondage, 9–10, 12, 47, 50, 69–86, 96–98, 101, 107, 109–10, 115

Pentecost *(Shavuot)*, 107

Phineas, 130

Pirke deRabbi Eliezer, 48

Prayer: of Supplication, 170, 174; and synagogue life, 167–93

Psalms for Grace after Meals, 33–34

Public affairs, *see* Community life

Rab, 155

Rashi, 55, 216

Rava, 120

Redemption: festivals of, 85–99; Judaism of Holocaust and, 21–22, 24–26, 194–204

Religion: contemporary Judaism and world view of, 13–28; of dual Torah and Holocaust and Redemption, 194–204; role of, in life of world, 3–12; and Temple cult and family purity of meals, 34–37

Rosh Hashanah, 9, 100–13

General Index

INDEX OF BIBLICAL REFERENCES

South Florida Studies in the History of Judaism